# THE CONVERSION OF CONSTANTINE

# THE
# CONVERSION
# OF CONSTANTINE

**Edited by JOHN W. EADIE**
*The University of Michigan*

**HOLT, RINEHART AND WINSTON**
New York • Chicago • San Francisco • Atlanta
Dallas • Montreal • Toronto • London • Sydney

Cover illustration: Constantine the Great. Head of a statue from the Basilica of Maxentius, now in the Palazzo dei Conservatori, Rome. *(Pan American Airways)*

Copyright © 1971 by Holt, Rinehart and Winston, Inc.
All Rights Reserved
Library of Congress Catalog Card Number: 73–113827
**SBN: 03–083645–X**
Printed in the United States of America
1 2 3 4   008   9 8 7 6 5 4 3 2 1

# CONTENTS

From a ninth-century Byzantine manuscript of the sermons of Gregory of Nazianzus. Upper panel, the dream of Constantine; center, the vision of Constantine; lower panel, Constantine's mother, St. Helena. *(Segalat)*

# INTRODUCTION

The phenomenon of religious conversion is abundantly attested in the historical literature of the Western world. Less well documented, however, are the motives of individual converts and the sincerity and intensity of their commitment to the new faith. Conversion, whatever its form, usually remains an exclusively personal experience, unnoticed and uncommemorated by outsiders. But when a prominent and influential "public man" affiliates with a new cult, accepts a new faith, or adopts a new life style, this intrinsically private decision may become a matter for public concern and comment. If the consequences of his conversion are thought by contemporaries to be important, it may acquire a place in historical literature. Occasionally the convert accelerates the process of historicization by submitting his own account in an autobiography (for example St. Augustine's *Confessions*) or a diary. More often, however, information concerning the conversion is supplied by others. Unfortunately these external accounts characteristically contain only part of the story. The consequences of the convert's action may be detailed at length, but a precise description of the events leading to conversion and an analysis of the individual's motives will rarely be included. Even when an author does make some effort to discuss motivation, we cannot assume that the analysis is correct, for his conclusions may be based on inadequate data, honest misinterpretation, or deliberate falsification. Accounts of religious conversion are especially susceptible to these familiar historiographical defects; correspondingly, to discover what really happened we must carefully test every statement. The wisdom of this skeptical approach is nowhere better illustrated than in the controversy over the alleged conversion of the Roman emperor Constantine to Christianity. For here the conversion under investigation occurred several millennia in the past, is reported by interested, not to say biased, observers, has been enshrined in the literature of an organized religion, and is generally considered one of the significant turning points in history. The selections included in this book explore the answers to two sets of questions regarding Constantine's religious actions: (1) Was Constantine converted to Christianity, and (2) if so, when, how, and above all why did he decide to accept the new faith?

As every student of biography knows, the actions and thoughts of a public man during his middle and later years may be recorded in some detail, while his youthful experiences are ignored completely or recounted in a series of random and fragmentary flashbacks. And so it is with Constantine. Constantine, of course, was never an obscure individual—his father was Constantius Chlorus, a member of the Tetrarchy[1]—but he clearly did not become a prominent and newsworthy figure until his decisive defeat of Maxentius at the Milvian Bridge (Ponte Molle) on October 28, 312.[2] Most of our information about his early life was assembled after this event, and comes from Christian writers, who naturally were more interested in praising the "Christian" emperor than in examining the details of his pagan youth. The only indisputable evidence regarding his religious thinking before 312 is provided by a pagan panegyrist; namely, that in 310 Constantine apparently became a devotee of Apollo, whom he may have considered another manifestation of Sol Invictus (the "Unconquered Sun"), the eastern deity favored by his father. Thus Constantine evidently worshiped pagan gods down to the year 312 at least, and was not affiliated in any way with the Christian Church—although he, like his father, did not participate in the persecution of Christians.

The history of church-state relations before 312 certainly does not suggest that a détente, still less an outright espousal of the Christian cause by the emperor, was imminent or practicable. On the contrary, in the opening years of the fourth century the Christian community—which at that time probably comprised no more than 10 percent of the population residing within the Empire—had been vigorously persecuted by the co-Augusti of the Tetrarchy, Diocletian and Maximian. The immediate causes of this "Great Persecution" (A.D. 303–305) are not known with certainty, but it is quite clear that Diocletian and his colleagues intended through imperial decrees to eliminate Christianity as a viable religious option for Roman citizens. The repressive edicts were carried out most effectively in the eastern provinces, where mistrust of the historically militant Christian community was accentuated by local pagan-Christian disputes and was encouraged by political opportunists. Persecution in this region, even with the change of rulers after 305, continued sporadically until 311. In the West, on the other hand, animosity toward the Christians, who in any case were not considered a major political threat, was overshadowed by the civil war that followed the abdication of Diocletian and Maximian in 305. Between 305 and 312 control of the western provinces was contested by no less than six claimants, each of whom was supported by substantial armed forces. While political warfare consumed the energies of both rulers and rivals, the Christian Church enjoyed a period of relative peace.

Following the defeat of Maxentius in 312 this *de facto* toleration was recognized officially in the universal edict of toleration issued by the new co-Augusti, Constantine and Licinius—the so-called Edict of Milan, in fact a ratification of

---

[1] The Tetrarchy—four co-rulers, two Augusti assisted by two Caesars—was introduced by Diocletian in A.D. 293.

[2] Maxentius was the son of Maximian (emperor-Augustus of the West from 293 to 305). Excluded from the Tetrarchy, Maxentius rebelled in 306 and controlled Italy until October 28, 312.

the decree published by the eastern emperor Galerius in 311—which legalized Christianity and in effect protected Christians against arbitrary persecution. Between October 312 and October 314 (when the battle of Cibalae ended the "first civil war" between Constantine and Licinius) this edict was reinforced by imperial legislation granting certain privileges to the Christian church. Although Constantine clearly was the moving force behind this legislation, there is no reason to believe that Licinius opposed these concessions to the Christians. There is, in fact, no evidence of religious schism at this time. With the outbreak of the "first civil war" in 314 and the corresponding increase in political hostility, however, religious rivalry developed. By the time of the battle of Chrysopolis (September 18, 324), which marked the end of the "second civil war," politics and religion had become so entangled that contemporary observers could describe Constantine's political attack on Licinius as a crusade against paganism and its spokesman. Thus, by accident or by design, Constantine emerged from the battle of Chrysopolis not only as the sole ruler of the Empire, but also as the new champion of the Christian faith.

Was Constantine now a Christian? If so, when did his conversion occur? To what extent did his experience before or during the battle at the Milvian Bridge influence his decision to adopt Christianity? Investigation of these questions must begin with the three literary accounts of the events of October 312, which are reproduced below.

The insecure nature of ancient literary "sources" is succinctly illustrated in these accounts. None was written by an eyewitness to the events described, and all were composed years or even decades later by committed Christians, who frequently subordinated their critical faculties to the demands of providential history. Not surprisingly, their narratives often reflect the motives and methodology of Christian apologetic literature. The earliest of these accounts (*ca.* 315) is contained in book nine of the *Ecclesiastical History* written by Eusebius, the learned and disputatious bishop of Caesarea and after 325 an influential member of Constantine's court. His is the shortest of the three major accounts and uniquely omits any reference to a dream or vision experienced by the emperor at the time of the battle of the Milvian Bridge. Eusebius nonetheless clearly indicates that Constantine achieved his victory over Maxentius with the aid of the Christian God. In Eusebius' opinion, Constantine was a Christian, or was at least cognizant of the power of Christ, after October 312.

Lactantius, tutor to Constantine's son Crispus, provides a rather different version in his pamphlet *On the Deaths of the Persecutors*. This celebration of the end to the persecution and the demise of all those responsible for the repression was composed after 313, but the precise date of the completion is not certain—most scholars prefer a date around 318. According to Lactantius, Constantine was admonished in a dream on the eve of the battle to inscribe the "heavenly sign of [the Christian] God" on his soldiers' shields. Equipped with this talisman and assisted by the Christian God, Constantine defeated Maxentius. In Lactantius' judgment this divine intervention marks the beginning of a new day for the Christian church; hereafter, the purposes of Constantine and the Christian God would be identical.

The third and by far the most detailed literary account is found in the *Life of Constantine,* an enthusiastic and scarcely impartial biography, replete with miracles and providential interventions, which has long stimulated scholarly imagination and debate. Is the *Life* from the pen of Eusebius or is it a baroque fantasy concocted by an unknown Christian writer in the second half of the fourth century? Are the multifarious "documents" contained in it authentic? These problems are relevant to our topic, for belief in the genuineness of Constantine's conversion has traditionally been based on the account in the *Life.* If the *Life* contains spurious documents or was produced in the late fourth century from demonstrably second-hand information, the historical value of its version of Constantine's experiences in October 312 may be seriously questioned. The key elements in this account are the description of the miraculous vision and the subsequent dream, the suggestion that the meaning of the vision was revealed to Constantine by Christian interpreters, and the statement that the author obtained his information from Constantine himself.

Can we hope to discover the truth concerning the events of October 312 in these tendentious and frequently contradictory accounts? Is their testimony, in any case, essential to our understanding of Constantine's actions? Concentration on these possibly unreliable narratives may seem unenlightened and unnecessary in this era of the artifact, especially since we possess nonliterary evidence—inscriptions, coins, *objets d'art*—which may be used to amplify or correct the literary record. But it must be remembered that these data also are scraps, fragments of the story, usually unconnected and of uneven quality. For this reason scholars have generally affirmed the primary importance of the literary accounts, even when they could not accept their contents. Lactantius' pamphlet, Eusebius' *History,* and the *Life,* together with the pagan panegyrics, have been the starting point for all discussions of the conversion and the foundation of most modern interpretations of Constantine's religious policies. Even with the addition of nonliterary data, the fact remains that the literary sources provide the only continuous and contextual narrative of Constantine's religious attitudes and development. Indeed, if they did not exist, there would not be sufficient material for controversy.

When Edward Gibbon composed his interpretation of the conversion, contained in his famous *Decline and Fall of the Roman Empire,* most of the nonliterary data had not been uncovered or assessed. Thus Gibbon was forced to rely almost exclusively on the literary accounts, supplemented by a few coins and the inscription on the Arch of Constantine. Employing "reason," buttressed by a preconceived mistrust of the miraculous, Gibbon attempted to separate "the historical, the natural and the marvellous parts of this extraordinary story, which . . .

have been artfully confounded in one splendid and brittle mass." Three prominent features of the literary accounts were correspondingly selected for analysis: the standard (labarum), the dream, and the celestial sign (the vision of the cross). That his interpretation of the ancient testimony still merits careful consideration is a tribute to Gibbon's remarkable historical skill.

Since the publication of Gibbon's synthesis, three interpretations of the conversion have dominated historical literature: That Constantine was never a sincere Christian and pretended to accept the new faith for purely political reasons; that he considered the Christian god merely another member of his syncretic pantheon, which was devised to support his claim to universal monarchy; that his conversion to Christianity was genuine and subsequently determined his religious policies. The selections included in this book, arranged in order of publication within each group, represent significant stages in the development of each interpretation and have been chosen primarily because they are the most recent— Burckhardt is an obvious exception—and innovative contributions to the controversy. The reader will quickly observe that the main arguments were delineated in the 1930s; the majority of recent examinations draw heavily on work published in that decade.

Jacob Burckhardt was not the first to portray Constantine as a calculating politician—Gibbon, for example, refers to detractors who argued that Constantine "used the altars of the church as a convenient footstool to the throne of the empire"—but he contributed more than anyone else to the popularization of this view. Burckhardt's Constantine is a thoroughly political individual, a skillful manipulator of armies and public opinion, the natural offspring of an age of convulsive political competition. His thesis is predicated on two premises: (1) that the Christians had become a significant political force by the end of the third century and could be employed by shrewd politicians in their quest for power; (2) that the *Life of Constantine,* which Burckhardt considered an authentic Eusebian panegyric, intentionally and cleverly concealed the real Constantine. The reader must decide whether Burckhardt uncovered the real Constantine, lost for centuries through Eusebius' distortions, or simply made Constantine conform to the pattern of rational behavior which was expected of a nineteenth-century politician.

Among the twentieth-century proponents of the political interpretation Henri Grégoire was certainly the most provocative. His article "The Conversion of Constantine"—a portion of which is reproduced here—redefined the controversy. Like Burckhardt, Grégoire believed that the ancient literary accounts were misleading and must be subjected to rigorous cross-examination. Repeatedly he drew attention to three crucial historiographical problems: (1) the authorship of the *Life of Constantine* and the authenticity of the documents contained in it; (2) the discrepancies between the account of the "Christian vision" in Lactantius' pamphlet and that in the *Life of Constantine;* and (3) the relationship between Constantine's "pagan vision" in the Gallic sanctuary, reported by the pagan panegyrists, and the "Christian vision" before the Milvian Bridge, reported by Christian writers. Inevitably, many scholars have disagreed with his overall interpretation of Constantine's religious attitudes, but few have denied the value of his trenchant critique of the ancient sources.

Grégoire's attack on the credibility of the *Life* is rightly considered his greatest contribution to the conversion controversy, but his examination of the relationship between the "pagan" and the "Christian" visions is scarcely less important. For Grégoire, Constantine's encounter with Apollo in the Gallic sanctuary (310), described by the pagan author of the panegyric delivered at Trèves (Trier) in 310, confirmed his thesis that the "Christian" vision was a gigantic hoax. The derivative character of the Christian vision is also accepted by Jean-Jacques Hatt, who argues that the sign described by Lactantius and the author of the *Life* is simply an adaptation of an existing Celtic symbol. According to Hatt, Celtic associations—facilitated by the political ties of Constantine's family with the region and strengthened by the Gallic contingent in his army—exercised considerable influence on Constantine's religious thinking, as his pagan "conversion" in 310 indicates. The real significance of this pagan vision lies not in Constantine's acceptance of Sol-Apollo as a personal deity, but in the opportunity for manipulation of public opinion offered by the Celtic symbols connected with his cult.

Grégoire and Hatt are not alone in emphasizing the pagan vision, but their "political" interpretation of the event differs markedly from the view of those who see in both the pagan vision of 310 and the Christian vision of 312 evidence of Constantine's syncretic tendencies. This alternative hypothesis is represented here in the selection by André Piganiol, who stresses throughout the evolutionary nature of the emperor's attitudes. While he argues that the encounter with Sol-Apollo constitutes "the only authentic vision of Constantine," Piganiol does not discount the influence of "the cult of the cross" on Constantine's religious development. The syncretic explanation, he suggests, is entirely consistent with the evidence (nonliterary as well as literary) and with what we know of Constantine's character and of fourth-century conditions.

With the selection by Jacques Moreau we return to the central source problem: How reliable are the literary accounts of Constantine's conversion to Christianity? Here Moreau attempts to prove that these reflect Constantine's propaganda on the eve of the second war against Licinius and are not trustworthy; for example, it is "useless to search for any historical reality in Lactantius' account." His rejection of the Christian testimony, however, does not lead him to accept Grégoire's political hypothesis. Instead, Moreau believes that Constantine was content to accumulate heavenly patrons so long as these were effective in times of crisis and generally did not offend any of his supporters.

If we accept the verdict of the political and syncretic schools regarding the reliability of the literary accounts, must we conclude that Constantine did not adopt Christianity in 312? Perhaps not, if it can be demonstrated that Constantine's actions and statements in the decade or so following his supposed conversion unmistakably reflect his commitment to the Christian faith. This retrospective approach is employed by most of those who accept the reality and sincerity of Constantine's conversion to Christianity around 312. In their judgment, Constantine's actions between 312 and 324 not only confirm the fact of his conversion but also enhance the credibility of the ancient explanations of his decision to adopt Christianity. But even if his official policies toward the Christian religion after 312 were meticulously conciliatory, can we be certain that this benevolence was not politically inspired or part of a larger syncretic plan?

Recognizing that this question of motivation cannot be answered by the literary evidence alone, Norman H. Baynes, in his Raleigh Lecture of 1929, assembled and carefully assessed the "corroborative" data from the period 312–324 — the edicts favorable to the Christian Church, Constantine's personal mediation of Church disputes, and his religious pronouncements in the "documents." These documents, in Baynes' judgment, are authentic and trustworthy, despite the fact that most are found only in the *Life of Constantine*. Largely on the basis of these he concludes that Constantine's later actions are explicable only if we believe that he adopted Christianity in 312. J.-R. Palanque also accepts the genuineness of the Christian conversion, but asserts that this was only one of three sincere conversions. Palanque portrays Constantine as a superstitious individual who passed through several stages in his religious development: from solar mysticism to philosophic monotheism to superstitious Christianity. Constantine's credulity is also fundamental to Andreas Alföldi's interpretation. Employing as corroborative evidence the "impeccable documents" and the Christian legends which appeared on official coinage after 315, Alföldi argues that the vision reported in Lactantius' pamphlet and the *Life* is not an invention but a historical fact. The superstitious Constantine accepted the vision as a direct call from the Christian God and "embraced the Christian cause with a suddenness that surprised all but his closest intimates."

Alföldi was one of the first commentators to emphasize numismatic evidence in an interpretation of the conversion. His analysis of the legends on the coinage has been widely accepted, but another numismatist, Patrick Bruun, has recently reopened the question. After a comprehensive review of all the Constantinian coinage, he concludes that the legends and symbols on the coins do not prove that Constantine adopted Christianity. A second element in Alföldi's analysis, Constantine's superstitious nature, has also been reassessed by Ramsay MacMullen in the context of fourth-century magic and occult practices. His suggestion that the cross in this environment could be seen as just another talisman, which might bring good luck to the believer or counteract threatening magical spells, supplements Alföldi and should serve as an appropriate warning to those who interpret Constantine's motives in purely political or ecclesiastical terms.

Like Baynes and Alföldi, A. H. M. Jones bases his acceptance of Constantine's conversion to Christianity on documentary evidence from the period 312–324.

Especially decisive in his view are the letters to Caecilian and Anullinus, which are the "earliest evidence of Constantine's new attitude to the Church." This new attitude was the direct result of Constantine's vision, which Jones suggests was actually a rare occurrence of the halo phenomenon.

Literary accounts, dedicatory inscriptions, official coinage, imperial legislation—from these disparate sources the modern historian must construct his interpretation of Constantine's religious attitudes and policies. That few of the interpretations proposed in this book embrace all the data should not be surprising, for the historian is only required to select and emphasize those facts which, in his judgment, most satisfactorily explain the course of events. In assessing the selections, the reader should carefully evaluate the principles which determine these individual choices, for it is in this process of selection that objectivity frequently surrenders to personal preconceptions. Above all, one should not lose sight of the larger problem: If Constantine adopted either the cult of Sol-Apollo or Christianity, *why* did he do so. Do any of the selections provide a convincing answer to this question? Admittedly, it may seem a matter for psychoanalytic rather than historical inquiry. But, despite some notable advances in the application of psychoanalytic methods to historical problems, it is unlikely that we have sufficient material for the delineation of Constantine's psychological profile. This would require, among other things, a much larger collection of Constantine's own writings than we now possess. In the end the historian will rely on the empirical techniques of his trade; indeed, the problem provides a good test of traditional historical methodology. That reasonable success can be achieved within these limitations is demonstrated by the recent synthesis of Joseph Vogt, a portion of which is reproduced here.

Whatever one decides regarding Constantine's motives or the historicity of his conversion to Christianity there can be no doubt that he established a tolerant environment in which Christian views could be disseminated with impunity. Moreover, his decision to favor the Christian Church through imperial legislation provided the Church with a powerful patron and guaranteed that its enhanced patrimony would be respected in future. In short, although Christianity did not become the official state religion until the reign of Theodosius I, Constantine's "conversion" dramatically accelerated the Christianization of the Roman Empire. It thus merits a prominent place among the significant events of Western history.

In the reprinted selections, footnotes appearing in the original sources have in general been omitted unless they contribute to the argument or better understanding of the selection.

The remarkable burst of literary activity in the fourth century, which has led some scholars to describe this period as the "first renaissance," was stimulated in large measure by the feverish competition between the pagan establishment and the Christian church. Among the most conspicuous and prolific champions of the Christian cause was EUSEBIUS of Caesarea (A.D. ?260–?340), bishop of his native city from A.D. 311 and adviser to the emperor Constantine after the defeat of Licinius. In the *Ecclesiastical History,* as in most of his other works, Eusebius jubilantly condemns deceased or dethroned enemies of the Church—especially Galerius, whose persecution Eusebius witnessed in Palestine between 306 and 311—and provides a retrospective assessment of the role of Providence in Roman history. Originally written in 315 and revised ten years later, the following selection from the *Ecclesiastical History* gives the earliest literary account of Constantine's conversion to Christianity.*

**Eusebius**

# *Ecclesiastical History*

Constantine, the superior of the Emperors in rank and dignity, was the first to take pity on those subjected to tyranny at Rome; and, calling in prayer upon God who is in heaven, and His Word, even Jesus Christ the Saviour of all, as his ally, he advanced in full force, seeking to secure for the Romans their ancestral liberty. . . . The Emperor [Constantine], closely relying on the help that comes from God, attacked the first, second and third of the tyrant's armies, and capturing them all with ease advanced over a large part of Italy, actually coming very near to Rome itself. Then, that he might not be compelled because of the tyrant to fight against Romans, God Himself as if with chains dragged the tyrant far away from the gates [of Rome]. . . . As, for example, in the days of Moses himself and the ancient and godly race of the Hebrews, "Pharaoh's chariots and his host hath he cast into the sea, his chosen horsemen, even captains, they were sunk in the Red Sea, the deep covered them"; in the same way also Maxentius and the armed soldiers and guards around him "went down into the depths like a stone," when he turned his back before the God-sent power that was with Constantine and was cross-

*From Eusebius, *The Ecclesiastical History* (IX, 9, 2–10), the Loeb Classical Library edition translated by K. Lake and J. E. L. Oulton, volume 2 (London, 1932), 359–365. Reprinted by permission of the publisher, Harvard University Press.

ing the river that lay in his path, which he himself had bridged right well by joining of boats, and so formed into an engine of destruction against himself. . . .

Thus verily, through the breaking of the bridge over the river, the passage across collapsed, and down went the boats all at once, men and all, into the deep; and first of all he himself, that most wicked of men . . . sank as lead in the mighty waters. . . . [Constantine] entered Rome with hymns of triumph, and all the senators and other persons of great note, together with women and quite young children and all the Roman people, received him in a body with beaming countenances to their very heart as a ransomer, saviour and benefactor, with praises and insatiable joy. . . . And straightway he gave orders that a memorial of the Saviour's passion should be set up in the hand of his own statue; and indeed when they set him in the most public place in Rome holding the Saviour's sign in his right hand, he bade them engrave this very inscription in these words in the Latin tongue: "By this salutary sign, the true proof of bravery, I saved and delivered your city from the yoke of the tyrant; and moreover I freed and restored to their ancient fame and splendor both the senate and the people of the Romans."

LACTANTIUS (A.D. ?250–?320), a native of the province of Africa and tutor to Constantine's son Crispus, was converted to Christianity late in life. Removed from his post as professor of rhetoric because of his Christian affiliation, Lactantius became an indefatigable critic of paganism and an ardent defender of the persecuted Christian church. His *On the Deaths of the Persecutors*, probably completed in 318, testifies both to his considerable literary skill and to his belief in providential history. Included in this work, a portion of which is reproduced here in translation, is the first reference to Constantine's vision at the Milvian Bridge—a divine intervention which, according to Lactantius, guided Constantine to victory over Maxentius.*

**Lactantius**

# *On the Deaths of the Persecutors*

Already the civil war between them [Constantine and Maxentius] had been set in motion. And although Maxentius remained in Rome, because an oracle had warned that he would die if he ventured outside the gates of the city, the war was being conducted by their capable commanders. Maxentius had a numerical advantage because he had received his father's army from Severus[1] and recently had raised his own composed of Mauri and Gaetuli. At the beginning of the struggle Maxentius' forces were winning, until Constantine, redoubling his courage and prepared for either death or victory, moved his army nearer the city and set up camp in the region of the Milvian Bridge. The anniversary of the day on which Maxentius had assumed the purple was at hand, that is the sixth day before the Kalends of November [October 28],[2] and the [celebrations of the] quinquennalia were ending. Constantine was admonished in a dream to inscribe on the shields [of his men] the heavenly sign of God and thus to commit himself to battle. He obeyed and inscribed [the sign of] Christ on the shields: the [Greek] letter X intersected by the [Greek] letter I, bent at the top. Armed with this sign the army took up their swords. The enemy, without a commander, advanced to meet them and crossed the bridge. The two lines, equal

---

[1] Severus acquired the army of Maximian (Maxentius' father) when he became Augustus of the West in 306.—Ed.

[2] Maxentius rebelled ("assumed the purple") on October 27 or 28, 306.—Ed.

---

*Lactantius, *On the Deaths of the Persecutors* (44, 1–11), edited by Jacques Moreau (Paris, 1954), pp. 126–128. Translated by John W. Eadie.

in length, came together and on both sides the battle was fought with the greatest vigor: "On neither side was flight considered."

There was discord in the city and Maxentius was rebuked as a traitor to public safety. When he was observed—for he was presiding at the circus on his anniversary—the people with one voice suddenly cried out that Constantine could not be defeated. Disturbed by this outcry, he hurried away and, calling together some of the senators, ordered that the Sibylline books be consulted: in them it was discovered that on that very day an enemy of the Romans would perish.

Misled by this oracle in the hope of victory, Maxentius went out and engaged in battle. The bridge was destroyed behind him. At this sight the fighting increased and the hand of God passed over the battlefield. The army was frightened and Maxentius himself, seeking safety in flight, hurried to the bridge, which had been destroyed; pushed along by the multitude of those fleeing, he was driven into the Tiber. Finally, when this most grievous war had ended, the emperor Constantine, received with great joy by the Senate and the Roman people, learned of Maximinus'[3] treachery—he discovered [incriminating] letters and found statues and busts. The Senate, in recognition of his bravery, bestowed on Constantine the title of Augustus, which Maximinus had claimed for himself. . . .

---

[3] Maximinus became a Caesar (under Galerius) in 308 and Augustus of the East in 311; in April 313 he was defeated by Licinius and died in August or September 313.—Ed.

The most elaborate, and at the same time the most controversial, account of Constantine's decisive battle with Maxentius is contained in the *Life of Constantine*. Most scholars now believe that Eusebius of Caesarea wrote the *Life* shortly before his death *ca.* 340, but there is a sizable and vocal minority who argue that the *Life* was composed in the latter half of the fourth century or at the beginning of the fifth by an inventive and unreliable Christian apologist. Advocates of both views agree, however, on one point: The *Life* provides "unique" information regarding the events leading up to the battle at the Milvian Bridge.*

**Eusebius(?)**

# Life of Constantine

[Constantine] said that life was without enjoyment as long as he saw the imperial city [Rome] thus afflicted, and prepared himself for the overthrow of the tyranny. Being convinced, however, that he needed some more powerful aid than his military forces could afford him . . . he sought Divine assistance. . . . He considered, therefore, on what God he might rely for protection and assistance. . . . [After all the options had been considered he] felt it incumbent upon him to honor his father's God[1] alone. Accordingly he called on him with earnest prayer and supplications that he would reveal to him who he was, and stretch forth his right hand to help him in his present difficulties. And while he was thus praying, a most marvelous sign appeared to him from heaven, the account of which it might have been difficult to believe had it been related by any other person. But since the victorious emperor himself long afterwards declared it to the writer of this history, when he was honored with his acquaintance and society, and confirmed his statement by an oath, who could hesitate to accredit the relation, especially since subsequent testimony has established its truth? He said that about noon, when the day was already beginning to decline, he saw with his own eyes the trophy of a cross of light in the heavens, above the sun, bearing the inscription "In this Conquer."

---

[1] Sol Invictus, the "Unconquered Sun."—Ed.

*Adapted from Eusebius, *Life of Constantine* (I, 26–40), translated by E. C. Richardson, in *A Select Library of Nicene and Post-Nicene Fathers of the Christian Church,* 2nd series (New York, 1890), vol. 1, pp. 489–493.

At this sight he himself was struck with amazement, as was his whole army, . . . which witnessed the miracle. . . . And while he continued to ponder its meaning, night suddenly came on; then in his sleep the Christ of God appeared to him with the same sign which he had seen in the heavens, and commanded him to make a likeness of that sign . . . and to use it as a safeguard in all engagements with his enemies. . . .

Now it was made in the following manner. A long spear, overlaid with gold, formed the figure of the cross by means of a transverse bar laid over it. On the top of the whole was fixed a wreath of gold and precious stones; and within this, the symbol of the Savior's name, two letters indicating the name of Christ by means of its initial characters, the letter P being intersected by X in its center:[2] and these letters the emperor was in the habit of wearing on his helmet at a later period. . . . Being struck with amazement at the extraordinary vision, and resolving to worship no other God save Him who had appeared to him, he sent for those who were acquainted with the mysteries of His doctrines, and inquired who that God was, and what was intended by the sign in the vision he had seen. They affirmed that He was God, the only begotten Son of the one and only God. . . .

Assuming therefore the Supreme God as his patron, . . . and setting the victorious trophy, the salutary symbol, in front of his soldiers and body-guard, he marched . . . against the first, second, and third divisions of the tyrant's forces, defeated them all with ease at the first as-

sault, and made his way into the very interior of Italy. And already he was approaching very near Rome itself, when . . . God himself drew the tyrant, as it were by secret cords, a long way outside the gates. . . . [Maxentius] essayed to cross the river which lay in his path, over which, making a strong bridge of boats, he had framed an engine of destruction. . . . Under divine direction, the machine erected on the bridge, with the ambuscade concealed therein, giving way unexpectedly before the appointed time, the bridge began to sink, and the boats with the men in them went to the bottom. . . .Constantine entered the imperial city in triumph. And here the whole body of the senate, and others of rank and distinction in the city . . . along with the whole Roman populace, . . . received him with acclamations and abounding joy. . . .

By loud proclamation and monumental inscriptions he made known to all men the salutary symbol, setting up this great trophy of victory over his enemies in the midst of the imperial city, and expressly causing it to be engraven in indelible characters, that the salutary symbol was the safeguard of the Roman government and of the entire empire. Accordingly, he immediately ordered a lofty spear in the figure of a cross placed beneath the hand of a statue representing himself, in the most frequented part of Rome, and the following inscription to be engraved on it in the Latin language: "By virtue of this salutary sign, which is the true test of valour, I have preserved and liberated your city from the yoke of tyranny. I have also set at liberty the Roman Senate and People, and restored them to their ancient distinction and splendour."

---

[2] The Greek letter *rho* intersected by the Greek letter *chi.*—Ed.

The following selection by EDWARD GIBBON (1737–1794) is a classic example of the rationalistic critique of Constantine's conversion. In assessing this account two factors should be kept in mind: (1) Gibbon, like many of his contemporaries, was a committed anticleric and a disbeliever in miracles; and (2) as much of the nonliterary data regarding the conversion was not available, Gibbon was forced to rely almost exclusively on the ancient accounts of Lactantius and the *Life*.*

**Edward Gibbon**

## *An Age of Religious Fervor*

In the general order of Providence princes and tyrants are considered as the ministers of Heaven, appointed to rule or to chastise the nations of the earth. But sacred history affords many illustrious examples of the more immediate interposition of the Deity in the government of his chosen people. The sceptre and the sword were committed to the hands of Moses, of Joshua, of Gideon, of David, of the Maccabees; the virtues of those heroes were the motive or the effect of the divine favour, the success of their arms was destined to achieve the deliverance or the triumph of the church. If the judges of Israel were occasional and temporary magistrates, the kings of Judah derived from the royal unction of their great ancestor an hereditary and indefeasible right, which could not be forfeited by their own vices, nor recalled by the caprice of their subjects. The same extraordinary providence, which was no longer confined to the Jewish people, might elect Constantine and his family as the protectors of the Christian world; and the devout Lactantius announces, in a prophetic tone, the future glories of his long and universal reign. Galerius and Maximin, Maxentius and Licinius, were the rivals who shared with the favourite of Heaven the provinces of the empire. The tragic deaths of Galerius and Maximin soon gratified the resentment, and fulfilled the sanguine expectations, of the Christians. The success of Constantine against Max-

*From Edward Gibbon, *The History of the Decline and Fall of the Roman Empire*, edited by J. B. Bury, vol. 2 (1896), chap. 20, pp. 295–307. Footnotes omitted.

entius and Licinius removed the two formidable competitors who still opposed the triumph of the second David, and his cause might seem to claim the peculiar interposition of Providence. The character of the Roman tyrant disgraced the purple and human nature; and though the Christians might enjoy his precarious favour, they were exposed, with the rest of his subjects, to the effects of his wanton and capricious cruelty. The conduct of Licinius soon betrayed the reluctance with which he had consented to the wise and humane regulations of the edict of Milan. The convocation of provincial synods was prohibited in his dominions; his Christian officers were ignominiously dismissed; and if he avoided the guilt, or rather danger, of a general persecution, his partial oppressions were rendered still more odious by the violation of a solemn and voluntary engagement. While the East, according to the lively expression of Eusebius, was involved in the shades of infernal darkness, the auspicious rays of celestial light warmed and illuminated the provinces of the West. The piety of Constantine was admitted as an unexceptionable proof of the justice of his arms; and his use of victory confirmed the opinion of the Christians, that their hero was inspired and conducted by the Lord of Hosts. The conquest of Italy produced a general edict of toleration; and as soon as the defeat of Licinius had invested Constantine with the sole dominion of the Roman world, he immediately, by circular letters, exhorted all his subjects to imitate, without delay, the example of their sovereign, and to embrace the divine truth of Christianity.

The assurance that the elevation of Constantine was intimately connected with the designs of Providence instilled into the minds of the Christians two opinions, which, by very different means, assisted the accomplishment of the prophecy. Their warm and active loyalty exhausted in his favour every resource of human industry; and they confidently expected that their strenuous efforts would be seconded by some divine and miraculous aid. The enemies of Constantine have imputed to interested motives the alliance which he insensibly contracted with the catholic church, and which apparently contributed to the success of his ambition. In the beginning of the fourth century the Christians still bore a very inadequate proportion to the inhabitants of the empire; but among a degenerate people, who viewed the change of masters with the indifference of slaves, the spirit and union of a religious party might assist the popular leader, to whose service, from a principle of conscience, they had devoted their lives and fortunes. The example of his father instructed Constantine to esteem and to reward the merit of the Christians; and in the distribution of public offices he had the advantage of strengthening his government by the choice of ministers or generals in whose fidelity he could repose a just and unreserved confidence. By the influence of these dignified missionaries the proselytes of the new faith must have multiplied in the court and army; the barbarians of Germany, who filled the ranks of the legions, were of a careless temper, which acquiesced without resistance in the religion of their commander; and when they passed the Alps it may fairly be presumed that a great number of the soldiers had already consecrated their swords to the service of Christ and of Constantine. The habits of mankind and the interest of religion gradually abated the horror of war and bloodshed which had so long prevailed among the Christians; and in the councils which were assembled under the gracious protection of Constantine the authority of the bishops was seasonably employed to ratify the obligation of the military oath, and to inflict the penalty of excommunication on those soldiers who threw away their arms during the peace of the church. While Constantine in his own dominions increased the number and zeal of his faithful adherents, he could depend on the support of a powerful faction in those provinces which were still possessed or usurped by his rivals. A secret disaffection was diffused among the Christian subjects of Maxentius and Licinius; and the resentment which the latter did not attempt to conceal served only to engage them still more deeply in the interest of his competitor. The regular correspondence which connected the bishops of the most distant provinces enabled them freely to communicate their wishes and their designs, and to transmit without danger any useful intelligence, or any pious contributions, which might promote the service of Constantine, who publicly declared that he had taken up arms for the deliverance of the church.

The enthusiasm which inspired the troops, and perhaps the emperor himself, had sharpened their swords while it satisfied their conscience. They marched to battle with the full assurance that the same God who had formerly opened a passage to the Israelites through the waters of Jordan, and had thrown down the walls of Jericho at the sound of the trumpets of Joshua, would display his visible majesty and power in the victory of Constantine. The evidence of ecclesiastical history is prepared to affirm that their expectations were justified by the conspicuous miracle to which the conversion of the first Christian emperor has been almost unanimously ascribed. The real or imaginary cause of so important an event deserves and demands the attention of posterity; and I shall endeavour to form a just estimate of the famous vision of Constantine, by a distinct consideration of the *standard*, the *dream*, and the *celestial sign;* by separating the historical, the natural, and the marvellous parts of this extraordinary story, which, in the composition of a specious argument, have been artfully confounded in one splendid and brittle mass.

I. An instrument of the tortures which were inflicted only on slaves and strangers became an object of horror in the eyes of a Roman citizen; and the ideas of guilt, of pain, and of ignominy, were closely united with the idea of the cross. The piety, rather than the humanity, of Constantine soon abolished in his dominions the punishment which the Saviour of mankind had condescended to suffer; but the emperor had already learned to despise the prejudices of his education and of his people, before he could erect in the midst of Rome his own statue, bearing a cross in its right hand, with an inscription which referred the victory of his arms, and the deliverance of Rome, to the virtue of that salutary sign, the true symbol of force and courage. The same symbol sanctified the arms of the soldiers of Constantine; the cross glittered on their helmet, was engraved on their shields, was interwoven into their banners; and the consecrated emblems which adorned the person of the emperor himself were distinguished only by richer materials and more exquisite workmanship. But the principal standard which displayed the triumph of the cross was styled the *Labarum,* an obscure, though celebrated, name, which has been vainly derived from almost all the languages of the world. It is described as a long pike intersected by a transversal beam. The silken veil which hung down from the beam, was curiously inwrought with the images of the reigning monarch and his children. The summit of the pike supported a crown of gold, which enclosed the mysterious monogram, at once expressive of the figure of the cross and the initial letters of the name of Christ. The safety of the labarum was intrusted to fifty guards of approved valour and fidelity; their station was marked by honours and emoluments; and some fortunate accidents soon introduced an opinion that as long as the guards of the labarum were engaged in the execution of their office they were secure and invulnerable amidst the darts of the enemy. In the second civil war Licinius felt and dreaded the power of this consecrated banner, the sight of which in the distress of battle animated the soldiers of Constantine with an invincible enthusiasm, and scattered terror and dismay through the ranks of the adverse legions. The Christian emperors, who respected the example of Constantine, displayed in all their military expeditions the standard of the cross; but when the degenerate successors of Theodosius had ceased to appear in person at the head of their armies, the labarum was deposited as a venerable but useless relic in the palace of Constantinople. Its honours are still preserved on the medals of the Flavian family.[1] Their grateful devotion has placed the monogram of Christ in the midst of the ensigns of Rome. The solemn epithets of safety of the republic, glory of the army, restoration of public happiness, are equally applied to the religious and military trophies; and there is still extant a medal of the emperor Constantius, where the standard of the labarum is accompanied with these memorable words, BY THIS SIGN THOU SHALT CONQUER.

II. In all occasions of danger or distress it was the practice of the primitive Christians to fortify their minds and bodies by the sign of the cross, which they used in all their ecclesiastical rites, in all the daily occurrences of life, as an infallible preservative against every species of spiritual or temporal evil. The authority of the church might alone have had sufficient weight to justify the devotion of Constantine, who, in the same prudent and gradual progress, acknowledged the truth and assumed the symbol of Christianity. But the testimony of a contemporary writer, who in a formal treatise has avenged the cause of religion, bestows on the piety of the emperor a more awful and sublime character. He affirms, with the most perfect confidence, that, in the night which preceded the last battle against Maxentius, Constantine was admonished in a dream to inscribe the shields of his soldiers with the *celestial sign of God,* the sacred monogram of the name of Christ; that he executed the commands of Heaven, and that his valour and obedience were rewarded by the decisive victory of the Milvian Bridge. Some considerations might perhaps incline a sceptical mind to suspect the judgment or the veracity of the rhetorician, whose pen, either from zeal or interest, was devoted to the cause of the prevailing faction. He appears to have published his Deaths of the Persecutors at Nicomedia about three years after the Roman victory; but the interval of a thousand miles, and a thousand days, will allow an ample latitude for the invention of declaimers, the credulity of party, and the tacit approbation of the emperor himself; who might listen without indignation to a marvellous tale which exalted his fame and promoted his designs. In favour of Licinius, who still dissembled his animosity to the Christians, the same author has provided a similar vision, of a form of prayer, which was communicated by an angel, and repeated by the whole army before they engaged the legions of the tyrant Maximin. The frequent repetition

---

[1] The Second Flavian dynasty, allegedly founded by Claudius II Gothicus, emperor 268–270.—Ed.

of miracles serves to provoke, where it does not subdue, the reason of mankind; but if the dream of Constantine is separately considered, it may be naturally explained either by the policy or the enthusiasm of the emperor. Whilst his anxiety for the approaching day, which must decide the fate of the empire, was suspended by a short and interrupted slumber, the venerable form of Christ, and the well-known symbol of his religion, might forcibly offer themselves to the active fancy of a prince who reverenced the name, and had perhaps secretly implored the power, of the God of the Christians. As readily might a consummate stateman indulge himself in the use of one of those military stratagems, one of those pious frauds, which Philip and Sertorius had employed with such art and effect. The praeternatural origin of dreams was universally admitted by the nations of antiquity, and a considerable part of the Gallic army was already prepared to place their confidence in the salutary sign of the Christian religion. The secret vision of Constantine could be disproved only by the event; and the intrepid hero who had passed the Alps and the Apennine might view with careless despair the consequences of a defeat under the walls of Rome. The senate and people, exulting in their own deliverance from an odious tyrant, acknowledged that the victory of Constantine surpassed the powers of man, without daring to insinuate that it had been obtained by the protection of the *gods*. The triumphal arch, which was erected about three years after the event, proclaims, in ambiguous language, that, by the greatness of his own mind, and by an *instinct* or impulse of the Divinity, he had saved and avenged the Roman republic. The Pagan orator, who had seized an earlier opportunity of celebrating the virtues of the conqueror, supposes that he alone enjoyed a secret and intimate commerce with the Supreme Being, who delegated the care of mortals to his subordinate deities; and thus assigns a very plausible reason why the subjects of Constantine should not presume to embrace the new religion of their sovereign.

III. The philosopher, who with calm suspicion examines the dreams and omens, the miracles and prodigies, of profane or even of ecclesiastical history, will probably conclude that, if the eyes of the spectators have sometimes been deceived by fraud, the understanding of the readers has much more frequently been insulted by fiction. Every event, or appearance, or accident, which seems to deviate from the ordinary course of nature, has been rashly ascribed to the immediate action of the Deity; and the astonished fancy of the multitude has sometimes given shape and colour, language and motion, to the fleeting but uncommon meteors of the air. Nazarius and Eusebius are the two most celebrated orators who, in studied panegyrics, have laboured to exalt the glory of Constantine. Nine years after the Roman victory Nazarius describes an army of divine warriors, who seemed to fall from the sky; he marks their beauty, their spirit, their gigantic forms, the stream of light which beamed from their celestial armour, their patience in suffering themselves to be heard, as well as seen, by mortals; and their declaration that they were sent, that they flew, to the assistance of the great Constantine. For the truth of this prodigy the Pagan orator appeals to the whole Gallic nation, in whose presence he was then speaking; and seems to hope that the ancient apparitions would now obtain credit from this recent and public event. The Christian fable of Eusebius, which, in the space of twenty-six years, might arise from the original dream, is cast in a much more correct and elegant mould. In one of the marches of Constantine he is reported to have seen with his own eyes the luminous trophy of the cross, placed above the meridian sun, and inscribed with the following words: BY THIS CONQUER. This amazing object in the sky astonished the whole army, as well as the emperor himself, who was yet undetermined in the choice of a religion: but his astonishment was converted into faith by the vision of the ensuing night. Christ appeared before his eyes; and displaying the same celestial sign of the cross, he directed Constantine to frame a similar standard, and to march, with an assurance of victory against Maxentius and all his enemies. The learned bishop of Caesarea appears to be sensible that the recent discovery of this marvellous anecdote would excite some surprise and distrust among the most pious of his readers. Yet, instead of ascertaining the precise circumstances of time and place, which always serve to detect falsehood or establish truth; instead of collecting and recording the evidence of so many living witnesses, who must have been spectators of this stupendous miracle, Eusebius contents himself with alleging a very singular testimony, that of the deceased Constantine, who, many years after the event, in the freedom of conversation, had related to him this extraordinary incident of his own life, and had attested the truth of it by a solemn oath. The prudence and gratitude of the learned prelate forbade him to suspect the veracity of his victorious master; but he plainly intimates that, in a fact of such a nature, he should have refused his assent to any meaner authority. This motive of credibility could not survive the power of the Flavian family; and the celestial sign, which the Infidels might afterwards deride, was disregarded by the Christians of the age which immediately followed the conversion of Constantine. But the catholic church, both of the East and of the West, has adopted a prodigy which favours, or seems to favour, the popular worship of the cross. The vision of Constantine maintained an honourable place in the legend of superstition till the bold and sagacious spirit of criticism presumed to depreciate the triumph, and to arraign the truth, of the first Christian emperor.

The protestant and philosophic readers of the present age will incline to believe that, in the account of his own conversion, Constantine attested a wilful falsehood by a solemn and deliberate perjury. They may not hesitate to pronounce that, in the choice of a religion, his mind was determined only by a sense of interest; and that (according to the expression of a profane poet) he used the altars of the church as a convenient footstool to the throne of the empire. A conclusion so harsh and so absolute is not, however, warranted by our knowledge of human nature, of Constantine, or of Christianity. In an age of religious fervour the most artful statesmen are observed to feel some part of the enthusiasm which they inspire; and the most orthodox saints assume the dangerous privilege of defending the cause of truth by the arms of deceit and falsehood. Personal interest is often the standard of our belief, as well as of our practice; and the same motives of temporal advantage which might influence the public conduct and professions of Constantine would insensibly dispose his mind to embrace a religion so propitious to his fame and fortunes. His vanity was gratified by the flattering assurance that *he* had been chosen by Heaven to reign over the earth: success had justified his divine title to the throne, and that title was founded on the truth of the Christian revelation. As real virtue is sometimes excited by undeserved applause, the specious piety of Constantine, if at first it was only specious, might gradually, by the influence of praise, of habit, and of example, be matured into serious faith and fervent devotion. The bishops and teachers of the new sect, whose dress and manners had not qualified them for the residence of a court, were admitted to the Imperial table; they accompanied the monarch in his expeditions; and the ascendant which one of them, an Egyptian or a Spaniard, acquired over his mind was imputed by the Pagans to the effect of magic. Lactantius, who has adorned the precepts of the Gospel with the eloquence of Cicero, and Eusebius, who has consecrated the learning and philosophy of the Greeks to the service of religion, were both received into the friendship and familiarity of their sovereign; and those able masters of controversy could patiently watch the soft and yielding moments of persuasion, and dexterously apply the arguments which were the best adapted to his character and understanding. Whatever advantages might be derived from the acquisition of an Imperial proselyte, he was distinguished by the splendour of his purple, rather than by the superiority of wisdom or virtue, from the many thousands of his subjects who had embraced the doctrines of Christianity. Nor can it be deemed incredible that the mind of an unlettered soldier should have yielded to the weight of evidence which, in a more enlightened age, has satisfied or subdued the reason of a Grotius, a Pascal, or a Locke.

The controversy over the conversion was both stimulated and popularized by JACOB BURCKHARDT (1818–1897) in his *Age of Constantine the Great,* from which the following selection is taken. In this rationalistic, yet impressionistic, survey Burckhardt attempts to demonstrate that Constantine was "essentially unreligious," a political opportunist invested with a Christian mission by the artful Eusebius. His case against the *Life of Constantine* rests on rational argumentation rather than on an analysis of conflicting evidence.*

**Jacob Burckhardt**

## *Eusebian Distortions*

Attempts have often been made to penetrate into the religious consciousness of Constantine and to construct a hypothetical picture of changes in his religious convictions. Such efforts are futile. In a genius driven without surcease by ambition and lust for power there can be no question of Christianity and paganism, of conscious religiosity or irreligiosity; such a man is essentially unreligious, even if he pictures himself standing in the midst of a churchly community. Holiness he understands only as a reminiscence or as a superstitious vagary. Moments of inward reflection, which for a religious man are in the nature of worship, he consumes in a different sort of fire. World-embracing plans and mighty dreams lead him by an easy road to the streams of blood of slaughtered armies. He thinks that he will be at peace when he has achieved this or the other goal, whatever it may be that is wanting to make his possessions complete. But in the meantime all of his energies, spiritual as well as physical, are devoted to the great goal of dominion, and if he ever pauses to think of his convictions, he finds they are pure fatalism. In the present instance men find it hard to believe that an important theologian, a scholar weak in criticism, to be sure, but of great industry, a contemporary as close as was Eusebius of Caesarea, should through four books repeat one and the same untruth a hundred times.[1] Men argue from

---

[1] Throughout Burckhardt is referring to the Eusebian(?) *Life of Constantine.* —Ed.

---

*From *The Age of Constantine the Great,* by Jacob Burckhardt. Published 1949 by Pantheon Books, a division of Random House, Inc. Reprinted by permission of Random House, Inc. and Routledge & Kegan Paul, Ltd. Pp. 292–300, 301–302, 304–306.

Constantine's zealous Christian edicts, even from an address of the Emperor "to the assembly of the saints," an expression impossible on the lips of a non-Christian. But this address, it may be remarked in passing, was neither composed by Constantine nor ever delivered; and in writing the edicts Constantine often gave the priests a free hand. And Eusebius, though all historians have followed him, has been proven guilty of so many distortions, dissimulations, and inventions that he has forfeited all claim to figure as a decisive source. It is a melancholy but very understandable fact that none of the other spokesmen of the Church, as far as we know, revealed Constantine's true position, that they uttered no word of displeasure against the murderous egoist who possessed the great merit of having conceived of Christianity as a world power and of having acted accordingly. We can easily imagine the joy of the Christians in having finally obtained a firm guarantee against persecution, but we are not obliged to share that elation after a millennium and a half.

Tolerant monotheism Constantine appears to have derived as a memory from the house of Chlorus,[2] who was devoted to it. The first definite notice of a religious act on the part of Constantine is his visit to the temple of Apollo at Autun (308) before his renewed attack upon the Franks. He appears to have consulted the oracle and to have made rich offerings. But this worship of Apollo does not necessarily contravene the monotheism of his parental home, for Chlorus conceived of the highest being as a sun-god. Constantine's nephew Julian speaks of Constantine's connection with a special cult of Helios. From a familiar obverse on coins of Constantine, representing the sun-god

with the inscription SOLI. INVICTO. COMITI [To our Comrade, the Unconquered Sun], we deduce that the personification of the sun as Mithras is here implied. Anyone who has dealt with ancient coins knows that out of five Constantinian pieces probably four will bear this obverse, so that there is high probability that this device was retained until the Emperor's death. Other devices which are frequent are Victories, the Genius Populi Romani, Mars and Jupiter with various epithets, and a number of female personifications. But the coins with unequivocal Christian emblems which he is said to have struck are yet to be found. In the period during which he ruled with Licinius the figure of the sun-god appears with the inscription COMITI. AVGG. NN., that is, "To the comrade of our two Augusti"; and many coins of Crispus and of Licinius himself bear the same obverse. On inscriptions and coins Constantine continually calls himself Pontifex Maximus, and has himself represented as such with head veiled. In the laws of 319 and 321 he still recognizes the pagan cult as existing as of right; he forbids only occult and dangerous practices of magicians and of haruspices [official diviners], but he admits conjurers of rain and hail, and on the occasion of public buildings being struck by lightning he expressly requests the responses of the haruspices. Zosimus, if we may credit that fifth-century pagan, confirms Constantine's consultation of pagan priests and sacrificers in even larger scope, and has them continue to the murder of Crispus (326), which, in his view, is the correct period of Constantine's supposed conversion.[3]

Opposed to all this is the fact that after the war with Maxentius (312) Constantine not only permitted the toleration of Christianity as a lawful religion, but

---

[2] Constantius Chlorus, Constantine's father.— Ed.

[3] Zosimus, pagan writer of the *New History* (flor. mid-fifth century).— Ed.

spread abroad in the army an emblem which every man could interpret as he pleased but which the Christians would refer to themselves. The interlocked letters X and P, which form the beginning of the word Christ (ΧΡΙΣΤΟΣ), were introduced on the shields of the soldiers, we are told, even before the war. At the same time or later the same emblem, surrounded by gold and jewels, was attached to a large battle standard, whereupon the sign received a special and remarkable cult and the soldiers were inspired with the greatest assurance of victory. Soon similar standards *(labarum, semeion)* were prepared for all armies, and a special guard was entrusted with the preservation of the emblem on the field of battle. The emblem even had its own tent, into which the Emperor mysteriously retired before any important affair. Should not all this signify an open profession?

First of all it is to be noticed that Constantine employed this sign not among the populace but in the army. The army knew him as a mighty and successful general from the time of the Frankish wars; it had descended to him largely from his father; and it was ready to accept any symbols or emblems he chose. Among the Gauls and Britons in the army there were certainly many Christians and indifferent pagans, and to the Germans the religion of their leader was a matter of no consequence. On his part it was an experiment that obliged him to nothing more than toleration, which was already in fact the rule in his previous domains and which he now extended to his conquests also. For him Christ may have rated as a god along with other gods, and the professors of Christ's religion along with the servants of the pagan deities. We shall not deny the possibility that Constantine developed a kind of superstition in favor of Christ, and that he may even have brought that name into

some kind of confused relationship with the sun-god. But without doubt he was concerned exclusively with success; if he had met with a powerful resistance against *XP* in Italy, the symbol would quickly have disappeared from shields and standards. Instead, he could now apparently be fully convinced that the great mass of pagans was displeased with the persecution and that he incurred no danger in setting up his statue, *labarum* in hand, in the midst of Rome and inscribing underneath it that this saving sign was the true proof of all courage. If he had wished to make a proper profession of Christianity, surely a very different sort of declaration would have been in place. A glance at the year 312 would make everything clear if we were better informed concerning general conditions. Nothing is more difficult to prove, and yet nothing is more probable, than that the temper of the pagans was more yielding and milder at the critical moment at the end of the persecution than either before or after. They did not know, or they forgot, that Christianity, once tolerated, must inevitably become the predominant religion.

Neither, perhaps, did Constantine know it, but he allowed it to come about, and he kept his eyes open. As soon as his lucid, empiric logic informed him that the Christians were good subjects, that they were numerous, and that the persecution could no longer have meaning in a reasonably governed state, his decision was taken. From the political point of view, the practical execution of his decision is wholly admirable. In his victorious hands the *labarum* was a physical representation at once of rule, of warlike power, and of the new religion. The *esprit de corps* of his army, which had been victorious over one of the greatest armies of ancient history, hallowed the new symbol with the aura of the irresistible.

But the familiar miracle which Eusebius and those who copy him represent as taking place on the march against Maxentius must finally be eliminated from the pages of history. It has not even the value of a myth, indeed is not of popular origin, but was told to Eusebius by Constantine long afterwards, and by Eusebius written up with intentionally vague bombast. The Emperor indeed swore a great oath to the bishop that the thing was not imagined, but that he actually saw in heaven the cross with the inscription "In this sign thou shalt conquer," and that Christ actually appeared to him in a dream, and the rest; but history cannot take an oath of Constantine the Great too seriously, because, among other things, he had his brother-in-law murdered despite assurances given under oath. Nor is Eusebius beyond having himself invented two-thirds of the story.

A great inconsistency in Constantine's outward bearing persists; he accepts the monogram of Christ as the emblem of his army and has the name of Jupiter on his triumphal arch erased, but at the same time he retains the old gods on his coins, and especially the sun-god as his unconquerable companion, and on important occasions his outward conduct is entirely pagan. This cleavage rather increases than decreases in his latter years. But he wished to give direct guarantees to both religions, and he was powerful enough to maintain a twofold position.

His edicts of toleration, of which the second, issued at Milan (313) in common with Licinius, is extant, confer nothing more than freedom of conscience and of religion; the latter granted freedom of worship without limitation and qualification. The notion of a state religion was thus abolished, until Christianity clothed itself with the shell which paganism had discarded. One regulation soon followed upon the heels of another, especially when Maximinus Daia in hostility to Li-

cinius and then Licinius himself in hostility to Constantine provoked the enmity of Christendom. The places of assembly and other landed property of the Christian communities which had been confiscated during the persecution were restored; the Christians were openly favored and their proselytization actively supported. A moment of anxiety because of the displeasure of the pagans is revealed in the laws of 319, cited above, in which the private practice of haruspices and home sacrifices are strictly forbidden, apparently because the secret consultation of haruspices and sacrificial feasts behind closed doors might be subversive politically. With the edict to the provincials of Palestine and with that to the peoples of the East after the last victory over Licinius (324), there follows an apparently quite unqualified personal devotion of the Emperor to Christianity, whose professors are freed of the consequences of the persecution with all possible indulgence, and are restored to their former position and property. These official decrees show a specifically polemic tone against polytheism; they speak of sanctuaries of falsehood, of darkness, and of miserable error which must still be suffered, and the like. But it is not Constantine's pen that wrote these things, though Eusebius maintains that he saw the autograph. The draftsman betrays himself at least in the second document, in which he has the Emperor say that he was "only a boy" at the beginning of the persecution, whereas in fact Constantine was almost thirty in 303. But indirectly the content is substantially the work of the Emperor, who, as is noticeable upon closer examination, does not once represent himself as a Christian. What personal tones are perceptible are those of the dreary deism of a conquerer who requires a god in order to justify his acts of violence by an appeal to something outside himself. . . .

It is not impossible that in his deism, originally derived from the sun and Mithras, Constantine believed that he possessed a more general and hence presumably a loftier basic configuration of all religions. At times he tried to find basically neutral expressions for religious practices which Christians and pagans alike should observe. Of this character is the common Sunday and the common Pater Noster.

He taught all armies zealously to honor the Lord's Day, which is also called the day of light and of the sun. . . . The pagans too were required to go forth into an open field on Sunday, and together to raise their hands, and recite a prayer learned by heart to God as giver of all victory: 'Thee alone we acknowledge as God and King, Thee we invoke as our helper. From Thee have we obtained our victories, through Thee conquered our enemies. Thee we thank for past favors, of Thee we hope for future favors. Thee we all beseech, and we pray Thee that Thou long preserve to us unharmed and victorious our Emperor Constantine and his God-loving sons.'

Christians would be content with this formula, and the pagans who might have taken offense at such outspoken monotheism were before all else soldiers. That special thought was taken for believers in Mithras also Eusebius indicates clearly with his "day of light and of the sun." How significant is this so-called prayer! Emperor, army, victory—and nothing else; not a word for moral man, not a syllable for the Romans.

Before we proceed further we may briefly dispose of Eusebius' other reports of the alleged Christianity of his hero. After the war with Maxentius Christian priests always attended him, even on journeys, as "assessors" and "table companions." At the synods he took his seat ın the midst of them. These facts are easily explained. It was essential for Constantine to have intelligence of the view-points of the contemporary Church; he had his own informants who delivered reports on the individual sects. With the eloquent reports of one of them, Strategius by name, he was so pleased that he gave him the cognomen Musonianus.[4] No clever and energetic ruler could let the praesidium of the synods out of his hands, for they were a new power in public life which it was unwise to ignore. One may deplore and contemn such egoism, but an intelligent power, whose origin is ambiguous, must of necessity act in this manner. When we are told further how frequently divine manifestations were vouchsafed the Emperor, how he secretly fasted and prayed in the tent of the *labarum,* how he daily shut himself in to converse with God on his knees, how he filled the watches of the night with thoughts on divine matters—on the lips of a Eusebius, who knew the truth, these things are contemptible inventions. In the later period Constantine was patently even more attentive to the bishops and gave them the first word at his court, apparently because he realized that it was to their greatest interest to support the throne in every way possible, and in the end because he could not do otherwise. In his encyclicals bishops are addressed as "beloved brother," and he himself affected to comport himself as one of them, "as a common bishop." He put the education of his sons, at least in part, in their hands, and in general so ordered matters that these sons should be regarded as unqualified Christians. Their personal environment, their court, consisted exclusively of Christians, whereas their father, by Eusebius' indirect admissions, did not hesitate to keep pagans in high positions about his person and as *praesides* [governors] in the provinces, along with the

---

[4] Derived from the Latin *Musa,* i.e. muse.—Ed.

clergy, until the last period of his life. The prohibition of gladiatorial games was doubtless a concession to his clerical environment, although the relevant law speaks only of "peace in the land and domestic quiet" for which bloody spectacles were not appropriate. In any case this was one of those laws which were promulgated only to fall straightway into oblivion, for Constantine himself later paid no attention to it.

The sermons which Constantine delivered from time to time in the presence of the court and "many thousands of auditors" are a complete puzzle. He wished, it is said, to prevail over his subjects "by discourses with edifying purpose" and "to make the reign one of discourse." Assemblies were convoked for this purpose, and the master of the world nonchalantly stepped forward and spoke. If he touched upon religion his gestures and voice took on an expression of deep humility. Applause he deprecated with a gesture toward heaven. His themes were usually refutation of polytheism, monotheism, providence, redemption, and divine judgment. In this section (the court bishop continues) he scored his auditors most directly, for he spoke of robbers, and men of violence, and the avaricious; the scourge of his words smote certain of his confidants who stood in attendance, so that they cast their eyes to the ground. . . . His intention was righteous, but they remained deaf and stubborn. They clamored their approval, but their insatiability suffered no emotion to stir within them. Constantine wrote these discourses in Latin, and interpreters turned them into Greek.—What are we to think of this account? Would Constantine, who preserved the Diocletianic fashion of imperial appearance so zealously, and who set such great store by his personal majesty, condescend to show himself before the crowds in the capital? The criticism

to which he would thus subject himself is the least of the problem, and perhaps his auditors would forgo criticism on very good grounds. But why speeches, when the Emperor possessed the fullest power to act? Perhaps one reason may be divined. In this period of religious crisis the spoken word, previously confined to rhetorical exercises and eulogies, now delivered from the preacher's pulpit, must have won so enormous an influence that Constantine could not entirely forgo it as an adjunct of power, just as the most powerful governments today must be represented in the periodical press. If it could occur to this unbaptized non-catechumen to give himself out as "a common bishop," he could equally well present himself as a Christian preacher. How he dealt with Christian dogma in these discourses we do not know; that he presented himself as an unqualified Christian is not even probable. . . .

It is precisely in the last decade of his life that Constantine gives certain very plain indications of un-Christian, even of directly pagan, sympathies. While he and his mother were ornamenting Palestine and the large cities of the Empire with magnificent churches, he was also building pagan temples in the new Constantinople. Two of these, of the Mother of the Gods and of the Dioscuri, may have been merely ornamental structures to house the idols which were preserved in them as works of art; but the temple and image of Tyche, the deified personification of the city, was intended to receive an actual cult. At the consecration of the city certain occult pagan practices were demonstrably celebrated; the solemnities involved superstitions of all sorts, which later writers vainly seek to identify with Christian worship. . . .

Even under Constantine, to be sure, temples were pulled down and destroyed and images melted down. A sanctuary like that of the Heavenly Goddess at Aphaka in the Lebanon deserved no better than that soldiers should be dispatched to raze it to the ground (about 330); the spot was in fact "unworthy that the sun shine upon it." More questionable was the razing of the famous Temple of Asclepius at Aegae in Cilicia, whither crowds of people had until that time resorted for the sake of curative dreams. Apparently the god ("the false guide of souls," Eusebius calls him) had become involved in political questions. At Heliopolis, whose cult was hardly less debauched than that of Aphaka, there was merely a prohibition and the enforced establishment of a bishopric, for which a congregation was then engaged for pay. Elsewhere it happened that converted populations pulled down local pagan sanctuaries of their own volition and then received official imperial approval. Probably as reward for such merits Majuma, the harbor city of Gaza, received the name of Constantia, and another Phoenician locality received the name of Constantina.

Constantine caused many temples to be plundered moreover, as it seems, out of desire for booty or need of pelf. Here too Eusebius dissembles the cause and the true extent of such spoliation, but he betrays himself unwittingly. For he does not speak of marble statues at all, but only of such whose interior consisted of some special material; Eusebius implies skulls, skeletons, old rags, hay, straw, and the like, but what is obviously intended are the wooden or other armatures that supported the hollow interiors of the so-called chryselephantine statues, that is, statues of gold and ivory, like that of the Zeus of Olympia. In his panegyric of Constantine this is fully avowed: "The valuable portions were melted down, and the amorphous remainder was left to the pa-

gans as a memorial of their reproach." What and how many statues (perhaps the finest in Greek art) met a fate inextricably involved in the value of their material we cannot know. For the decoration of his new capital, in any case, Constantine was very willing to use images whose material was of no great value, as we shall see. Of the brazen statues the same passage continues, "They were haled forth like captives, these gods of antiquated myth, they were dragged forth with ropes." Confiscation was in the hands of trusted commissioners, who came directly from the court. They encountered no resistance; priests were compelled to open their most secret crypts to them. But it is conceivable and not improbable that Constantine ventured such measures only in thoroughly reliable predominantly Christian cities in the near vicinity of the imperial residence. He might have left the statues of gold and silver untouched, but they were too convenient and the temptation was too great in the face of pressing financial need, which must take precedence over any other consideration in rulers of this sort. In the same category, doubtless, falls the removal of doors and beams, which is said to have taken place in the case of several temples; these members were often of massive bronze, and well worth the trouble of smelting. If this made a beginning of destruction and the interior was then injured by partial collapse and inclement weather, the inhabitants could hardly be prevented from venturing on columns and other structural members, if only for burning lime. We have official confirmation that such things happened after 333, at least to pagan grave monuments. Even earlier a law put a period to the repair of dilapidated or incompleted temples. How the temple properties fared is not precisely known; in individual cases they were certainly confiscated, but it was only under Constantine's successors that this was done in volume and systematically. It is out of the question that Constantine could have issued a law enjoining the general destruction of temples, as the *Chronicle* of Jerome reports for the year 335. What Constantine did or suffered to come about happened intermittently, out of frivolous desire for plunder and through the influence of the clergy, and hence his measures are not consistent. It is futile to seek for a logical system in a man who was intentionally illogical in this respect.

No one contributed more to research on the life and reign of Constantine than the late professor of Greek and Byzantine history in the University of Brussels, HENRI GRÉGOIRE (1881–1965). Unfortunately, the full-length study of Constantine which he promised never appeared, but its focus and thesis doubtless are reflected in his magisterial articles. In the selection printed here, from his article entitled "The Conversion of Constantine," the skeptical attitude toward the ancient literary sources and the overall interpretation of the conversion consistently recommended by Grégoire can be seen.*

Henri Grégoire

# *Everything But the Truth*

The Italian campaign of 312 abruptly changed the face of the Western world. The precise cause of this conflict between Constantine and Maxentius is not known. After the execution or suicide of Maximian [in 310] relations between Trèves and Rome were deplorable.... Was Maxentius responsible for the break? Was Constantine the "aggressor" in the meaning of the term in international law today? This is of little consequence. It is important, however, to know that religion was not an issue in this confict. Constantine had for a long time been rather favorably inclined toward the Christians—a little less so than Maxentius, it seems, for no one reports of him any measure of restitution, any intervention, paternal or not, in internal and Church activities. We are fairly well informed concerning his personal religion by the Gallic panegyrists, who were prevented by the constant law of their literary genre and plain good sense from expressing any thoughts on the nature of the gods likely to displease the young emperor. According to them, before 310 Constantine revered principally Hercules, patron of his grandfather Maximian Herculius, and after that time Apollo, to whom he remained faithful for a long time. No historical lie is more scandalous to the critical mind than the travesty of representing the campaign of 312 as a crusade.... Seeck places between April and August the capture of Susa (Segusio), the victory at Turin, the entrance into Mi-

*Henri Grégoire, "La Conversion de Constantin," *Revue de l'Université de Bruxelles,* 36 (1930), 231–272. Translated by John W. Eadie. Footnotes omitted.

lan, the brilliant success of the Gallic cavalry at Brescia, and the siege, assault, and capture of Verona; in September and October the conquest of Aquileia and Modena (Mutina). Everything has been said of the crowning victory of Saxa Rubra, or the Milvian Bridge (October 28). Everything, perhaps, but the truth. For this last battle was not waged under the sign of the cross any more than were the preceding ones. The panegyrists reproach Maxentius for many things: his cruelty toward the Senate and the people, his harassing taxes, the harshness of his police, his physical ugliness and moral baseness, in contrast to the Apollonian beauty and clemency of Constantine. But they accuse him above all of sacrilege: The tyrant of Rome, short of money, plundered the temples of the gods; consequently, the ancient Tiber carried him away in its avenging waters. It is believed that the panegyrists attribute the victory of their hero to the deity. But it is impossible to discern in their language the least allusion to a Christian miracle. The triumphal arch erected in 315, and decorated with various bas-reliefs representing among other pagan sacrifices the *suovetaurilia,*[1] speaks a neutral language: *instinctu divinitatis* [by the prompting of the divinity]. Lactantius, writing in 315–316, clearly states, in two lines, that Constantine was admonished in a dream, on the eve of the battle, to inscribe on the shields of his soldiers the sign of Christ, *transversa X littera, summo capite circumflexo* [the Greek letter *chi* intersected by the Greek letter *iota* bent at the top]. Here we have a monogram common enough in Asia Minor from the third century B.C. on, as the epigraphy of these provinces reveals; but is Lactantius' testimony credible? Before replying to this question, we must examine briefly a

passage in the *Life of Constantine,* generally put forward as confirmation of the *testimonium Caecilianum.*[2] Eusebius claims to have had a very detailed account from Constantine, who confirmed it under oath (*Life of Constantine* I, 28–30). This oath of Constantine has quite rightly made more than one critic suspicious. Without wishing to bring to this subject any sarcasm, Voltairean or otherwise, it is entirely justifiable to discard without argument the account in the *Life:* first because it is not a historical text but a romanticized panegyric; second and mainly because Eusebius does not mention in his *History* the prodigy described at such length in the *Life.* Moreover, the *Life* is in no way a contemporary source. According to the most generally held view and the one most favorable to this text, it dates from 337–340, at least a quarter of a century after the event. But today the most competent critics do not dispute the fact that the *Life* in its present form, published after the death of Eusebius, is a revised version, which contains material not in the original. No writer of the fourth century knew this work. St. Jerome did not include it in his catalogue of Eusebian works. To mention only these learned men — neither Basil nor Gregory of Nazianzus nor St. John Chrysostom[3] made use of it. As Gibbon has already seen, a letter of Cyril of Jerusalem, written after January 30, 351, provides decisive evidence against the authenticity of the vision of Constantine or at the very least proves that the *Life* had not yet been published at that time. Indeed, at the beginning of 351 (Mommsen, *Chronica minora,* I, p. 238) a bright meteor in the form of

---

[1] The *suovetaurilia* was a purification ritual. — Ed.

[2] The evidence adduced by Lactantius, whose full name was L. Caelius Lactantius Firmianus. — Ed.

[3] St. Basil (*ca.* 330–379), St. Gregory of Nazianzus (*ca.* 329–388), St. John Chrysostom (*ca.* 347–407). — Ed.

the cross appeared in the East, and contemporaries saw in this prodigy an omen of the decisive victory of Constantius II over Magnentius (battle of Mursa, September 28, 351). When Cyril of Jerusalem announced this prodigy to Constantius, he did not hesitate to tell him that the glorious vision with which he had been honored elevated him well above his father Constantine. For the latter had found the cross in the entrails of the earth, while Constantius had seen the salutary sign glittering in the sky in broad daylight—a much greater privilege, denied to Constantine. Puech does not doubt the authenticity of this letter . . . but, if it is apocryphal, that is to say if it dates from a certain number of years after 351, it is even more challenging to the authenticity of the *Life of Constantine,* whose appearance it would require us to defer until the end of the fourth century. An entire school, led by the great Gothofredus, formerly rejected the *Life,* and the reasons of these skeptics are not without weight. Relying on Cyril of Jerusalem, let us be content to say that more than forty years after the battle of the Milvian Bridge a great Palestinian bishop knew the legend of the finding of the cross by Constantine but had never heard of the miraculous vision, which was ignored by Eusebius himself in his *Ecclesiastical History.*

Furthermore, the account in the *Life of Constantine* does not seem in any way to refer to the same event as the "dream" of Lactantius. First, in the *Life,* everything takes place before the departure of the expedition for Italy, therefore in Gaul. Second, it is not in a dream but with his own eyes, at midday or rather in the early afternoon, that the emperor saw in the sky, above the sun . . . "the trophy of the cross, made of light, together with an inscription, 'Conquer by this.'" The dream, moreover, came next. The vision had oc-

curred during a march of the army, which collectively witnessed it; the following night (still in Gaul), Christ appeared in a dream to Constantine alone, with the celestial sign of the day before, in order to call upon him to reproduce it and to use it as a battle talisman. Upon waking, the emperor obeyed. Description of the new standard: According to a chapter heading known to be a post-Eusebian interpolation, it was the λάβαρον [labarum]. The high-flown description of the labarum need not detain us here. But let us note a final divergence from Lactantius. The monogram of Christ was not composed of the letters X and I, *summo capite circumflexo,* but of the letters X and P, the first two letters of the name of Christ.

These chapters of the *Life,* therefore, do not "confirm" Lactantius' account. At most they describe the last stage of a legend that originated in the time of Lactantius, but of which Lactantius himself did not give the first version. This legend in its original form was not Christian but pagan. It appeared first in Panegyric VII, delivered at Trèves around July 310, after the death of Maximian, by an orator from Autun. The orator recalls in the panegyric a vision of Constantine, who, on his way back from the campaign against Maximian Herculius, departed from his route in order to visit a temple of Apollo:

. . . I believe, Constantine, that you have seen your Apollo, accompanied by Victory, offering you laurel crowns, each of which carries the portent of thirty years of life. . . . But why say: I believe? You have witnessed it and have recognized yourself in the lineage of one to whom divine prophecies have promised world empire.

Nothing is better known than this symbol. Inscriptions on coins provide hundreds of examples for this period. These are the *vota publica* [public vows]. On the fifth anniversary of an emperor's reign the vows that had been addressed to the gods on his accession, petitioning a reign of five years, were fulfilled, and a reign of ten years was petitioned, VOTA V SIC X. For a tenth anniversary the formula was X SIC XX. For a twentieth, XX SIC XXX. But often the date of the anniversary was anticipated. In 310, ten years could be petitioned for Constantine, who was proclaimed at York in 306. And as J. Maurice points out, it also happened that in a delirium of enthusiasm the number of vows officially petitioned for the emperor might be greatly exceeded, and by far. So it was with our panegyrist who, like a good panegyrist, ignored all limits in wishing for the emperor, in advance, a reign not merely of ten, not merely of thirty, but of several times thirty years. . . .

Who can fail to see the striking similarity between the barred X [ ✳ ] placed in a laurel crown, which is one of the components of the Constantinian labarum, and the numeral sign X in a laurel crown, which is the common symbol of the *vota?* I have shown elsewhere that the word *labarum* itself is a simple distortion of *laureum,* for *laureatum* (the standard with the *laurea*). But let us not lose sight of the passage in Lactantius, which states that the soldiers inscribed the monogram on their shields. Nothing is more common on coins than the depiction of a shield on which the vows of the Roman people are inscribed. . . . One understands that the short passage in Lactantius gives a Christian interpretation of an official and military rite, admirably attested by the panegyrists and by coins. It is not only in 312, on the eve of the battle of the Milvian Bridge, but also several years earlier that Constantine's soldiers had to inscribe on their shields, sometimes in a circle recalling the *laurea,* the number X of the decennalian vows. This sign differs only by an iota from the monogram of Jesus Christ which had been in use for a long time in Asia Minor. From this time on Christian soldiers were able to add this iota without danger and even to interpret the official version of the vision of 309–310 in a way that would benefit their religion. Others could inscribe the sign ☧ all the more easily since it was susceptible of several interpretations sanctioned by the coinage: P(LURIMA) corresponded to the MULTA of the medallions; or better still, the V formed by the upper part of the X and the P which intersects the X called to mind the current legends VOTA PUBLICA, VICTORIA PRINCIPIS PERPETUA [the everlasting victory of the emperor], which are so common that I forgo citing references.

Constantine himself must have been struck by the manifold meanings of this symbol, which delighted the Christians without in the least troubling the pagans. And this is why he allowed Christianizing monograms to be engraved on certain of his coins from 317 on. He permitted this all the more readily as Maxentius before him had permitted [the Christians] to engrave a simple cross on coins in 311. Licinius figures here too: Some of his coinage and some coinage of his son Licinius Caesar carried, in 317, the letter T, equivalent of the cross, always in a laurel crown. Finally, Constantine placed the monogram in a crown at the top of the vexillum decorated with imperial portraits; but we are in 312, a period when one scarcely, and very hesitantly, begins to recognize the monogram of Christ in the number of the *vota publica.* Nothing as of this date permits us to speak of a conversion of Constantine.

JEAN-JACQUES HATT (b. 1913), professor in the University of Strasbourg, is an authority on the history of Gaul during Roman times. Not surprisingly his interest in Constantine centers on the emperor's experience in the Gallic sanctuary of Apollo in 310. Here Hatt assesses the significance of this encounter within the context of the Celtic symbolic system and suggests that this Celtic association exercised considerable influence on Constantine's religious attitudes and policies.*

Jean-Jacques Hatt

# Celtic Symbols

The origin of the Constantinian standard is a question still debated. The etymology proposed for the word *labarum,* that it was derived from *laureum,* raises difficulties. It is difficult to see how *laureum* could have been transformed phonetically into *labarum.*

Grégoire's studies showing the importance of the period before 312 and of the vision of 310 in the Gallic sanctuary in the creation of the Constantinian standard lead us to search for the origin of the labarum among the Celts.

The word is actually Gallic. In the *Punica* of Silius Italicus "Labarus" is given as the proper name of a Celtic general. *Labar* in Welsh *(Ilafar)* means "resonant, elo-

quent" and in Breton *(lavar),* "eloquence." The name for river, *Labara,* which has given rise to *Lièvre,* means "the resonant one, the roaring one."

The symbol itself is Celtic. One finds on certain Constantinian coins an aberrant form of the labarum, with the rectangular standard simply decorated with a cross in saltire (X), without the vertical spear, without the P of Christ's initials.

Furthermore, this sign, the cross in saltire, or St. Andrew's cross, on a rectangular field, is a Gallic religious symbol. . . . The Celtic St. Andrew's cross is nothing but the schematization of the wheel. The symbolism of the latter is twofold: It signifies sometimes the sun (no-

---

*Jean-Jacques Hatt, "La Vision de Constantin au sanctuaire de Grand et l'origine celtique du labarum," *Latomus* 9 (1950), 427–436. Translated by John W. Eadie. Footnotes omitted.

tably on tombstones) and sometimes the thunderbolt. In the hand of the "rider with serpent-footed [monster]," the thunderbolt probably is intended. In fact the special symbol of this last deity is, alternately, the wheel or the thunderbolt. . . .

Would not *labarum* then mean "resonant, roaring, terrible," because lightning, accompanied by thunder, was loud and terrifying? Was the Celtic standard originally an instrument of the war ritual intended to make a racket and by imitative magic to draw down the thunderbolt and its shafts on the enemy, to strike him or at least to terrify him, to surprise him? This calls to mind the shafts of lightning that appeared on shields or on sword sheaths of Roman soldiers. Actually these suppositions can be put forward only as hypotheses.

Be that as it may, it would have been a Celtic religious symbol, the X-shaped cross, that Constantine adopted following his sojourn in Gaul. It would have been this sign which led his soldiers, the great majority of whom were Gauls, to victory in 312, before a modification, in reality a very slight one, subsequently altered the St. Andrew's cross and made it into the initials of Christ.

Certain transitional forms, which are in fact extant, enable us to explain this transformation. They include a St. Andrew's cross intersected in the middle by a spear, with a dot or a wavy line above it. The last of these forms particularly can be construed as Sol's whip superimposed on the X-shaped cross. This would have been, in short, the *hasta capite circumflexo* [spear bent at the top] of which Lactantius speaks, and which would have been originally a syncretic, but still pagan, symbol.

Do the texts of the panegyrics warrant such an interpretation? The clearest and most important is the one that describes the pagan vision of Constantine in a Gallic sanctuary.[1]

Constantine had departed from Trèves in great haste in order to put down an insurrection in Arles fomented by Maximian. He had left Germany, but the threat of a barbarian invasion was about to force him to retrace his steps when he learned "that the flood [of invaders] had subsided" *(omnes fluctus resedisse)* and that calm had returned *(omnem quam reliqueras tranquillitatem redisse didicisti)*.

This turn of events induced him to give thanks to the gods to whom he had made vows *(ferre quod voveras)*. It is then that he visited—by making a detour which took him off the direct route from Trèves to Lyons—a Celtic sanctuary, the most beautiful in all the world *(templum toto orbe pulcherrimum)*, which was, according to all probability, situated at Grand.

Let us consider the historical importance of this course. At this moment Constantine had not yet been acknowledged as Augustus. He was at odds with Galerius. He had not agreed to proclaim in his territories his own consulate as a Caesar. He had asserted his independence by creating a new coinage in Gaul.

In seeking to realize his high ambitions, he was going to attempt first to rely on Gaul. His visit to the Gallic Apollo of Grand had an official and symbolic character. He went to pay his respects to the great god of the Celts and, at the same time, as we shall see, to request investiture from him.

In the sanctuary of Grand he beheld "his" Apollo, that is to say the solar god to whom he tended to assimilate himself, accompanied by Victory, holding out to him laurel crowns which promised him a reign of thirty years.

---

[1] Panegyric delivered in 311 at Trèves.—Ed.

The visual image which is the basis of this interpretation by the panegyrist has rightly been considered to have been three X's [XXX], three crosses in saltire encircled by laurel crowns.

Was this simply a subjective vision? The very words of the panegyric tend to prove that there was indeed present the display of a *genuine* divine group when Constantine recognized himself in the features of the deity.

There is probably a question here of a sculptured group which existed there, which Constantine saw, and whose appearance aroused his imagination.

We know that there was an important sanctuary of the Celtic Apollo at Grand. Two groups of the Gallic Jupiter come from Grand. One of these, now in the museum of Nancy, is well preserved. It is of a quite exceptional type. The serpent-footed monster, usually trampled under the horse's hoofs, is replaced here by a *winged Genius*. Is it not a sculpture of this kind which would have impressed Constantine and would have been the basis of the psychological shock mentioned by the panegyrist?

In view of its style, the group of Grand belongs at the end of the period of Gallo-Roman sculpture. It was discovered immured in a cistern. It doubtless still stood in or near the temple in Constantine's time. The rider-god appears there, holding in his right hand an object which has been lost: the shaft of a lance, some have suggested. But judging from the position of the hand, the object was held vertically. The lance, which is often seen in the hand of the Celtic Jupiter, is always thrust forward.

Was this not rather a banner?

Constantine went, then, to pay his respects to the Gallic Apollo of Grand. In the sanctuary he would have gazed upon a group with Jupiter as a Celtic rider, accompanied by a winged Genius or Victory and holding a variant of the ancient Celtic standard: the square *labarum*, ornamented with three crosses in saltire surrounded by laurel crowns.

Constantine would have recognized himself in this deity. He would have consented to be assimilated to him. The passage in the panegyric itself proves beyond doubt that from this moment in the eyes of the Gallic faithful identification had been made between the Apollonian prince "your Apollo," "your *numen*," and a Celtic deity "our Apollo."

It even seems that after this encounter between developed Celtic paganism and the syncretic pagan monotheism of Constantine, certain Gallo-Roman individuals attempted to draw the devotion of the prince to the local gods of Gaul. The panegyrist clearly expresses this in the following passage, which has not escaped the acuteness of Piganiol: *Iam omnia te vocare ad se templa videantur, praecipueque Apollo noster, cuius ferventibus aquis perjuria puniuntur, quae te maxime oportet odisse.* "Henceforth all the sanctuaries will seem to call you to them, principally our Apollo, who punishes perjurers with boiling waters, those perjurers whom you more than any other ought to hate."

Evidently there is a question here of an urgent invitation to sacrifice to the Gallic gods, based upon the precedent of Grand. The Apollo who punishes perjurers with boiling waters is the Apollo Borvo of the Gauls, god of hot springs, who had his sanctuary in Aeduan country, at Bourbon-Lancy. The allusion to the punishment of perjurers is singularly suggestive and seems to refer to some vow made by Constantine at the close of the visit to Grand, and to which he did not remain faithful. The Gauls had doubtless expected too much of Constantine's piety after the vision of Grand. He lavished gold upon the sanctuary and its priests. But what was merely the effect of a fortuitous encounter should not be taken for total allegiance to indigenous cults.

Further on the panegyrist invites Constantine, even more directly, to sacrifice to the Apollo of his country, god of springs, in the city of the Aeduans; he wished to see him kiss the miraculous waters, distribute presents, grant privileges in favor of this sanctuary, the seat of "his god" *(numinis tui sedem)*.

Constantine would accordingly have had, at this precise moment in 310, a vision assimilating him to the Celtic rider-god, bearer of the labarum. He would thus have received investiture from a Gallic deity. He would have become, in the eyes of the indigenous faithful, the incarnation of the god on earth. In view of this encounter certain individuals, among them our Aeduan orator, sought to win him over to the indigenous gods. They do not appear to have been successful. But the effect Constantine desired was achieved. The fervor of the Gallic masses was concentrated on his person; he could incorporate their particular mysticism into his theocratic system.

It is very probably that the idea of the labarum was born at this moment. The vision of the triumphant rider, of the symbolic standard, would have remained engraved in the imperial imagination. Besides, the prince had sensed the entire opportunity that existed for him in being identified with a Gallic god, "Our Apollo," in that critical moment of his career, when he absolutely needed the Gallic armies, reinforced by the loyalty of the civil population, in order to be able to set out, without anxiety and with every chance of success, on his conquest of the Empire.

In the year 310, then, he had been adopted by the Gauls as the incarnation of the native god. In fact, some time after the vision in the sanctuary at Grand and shortly before the Italian campaign, there seems to have been throughout Gaul an extraordinary burst of religious fervor, of which Constantine was the object. Hosts of cavalrymen were seen descending from the sky, who searched for Constantine, who had come to assist him. This collective hallucination was the repercussion, in the minds of the people, of the vision at Grand. The identification of Constantine with the Celtic Apollo had been enthusiastically received by the religious and loyal Gauls, who had always wanted to have an emperor truly their own. With political tension and rumors of war stirring them to a paroxysm of religious excitement, prodigies occurred. And these legions of cavalrymen were Celtic prodigies, a probable emanation from the will of the great Celtic god. After these new visions, which proved the intervention of the divine will, the Gauls had faith in Constantine's victory.

Constantine, who was never entirely converted to the Gallic religion, was carried away in an enthusiastic Celtic religious movement, in which he perhaps only halfway shared, but which singularly promoted his purposes. He could thus counter Maxentius' magic with other forms of divine conjuration, which he took from the Gallic ritual. He used this vague mysticism to his own ends. To urge his troops to the attack, to rouse them, to strengthen them in their trusting devotion, he was compelled to conform to their beliefs, to respect their symbolic system. He then gave them as emblem the labarum, the Celtic banner which would lead them to the final victory. Even if his personal convictions had from this moment led him toward Christianity, which remains in any case questionable, to impose a Christian emblem on his soldiers would have been incredible folly on his part. It is indeed, in all likelihood, the Celtic labarum, the simple St. Andrew's cross in a rectangle, which was inscribed on the shields and embroidered on the banner carried in advance of the legions.

In the midst of the battle of the Milvian Bridge and at the decisive moment, Constantine appeared to his soldiers in all his glory as divine emperor, in the guise of the Celtic rider-god. He insisted, in fact, on charging alone at the head of his troops. He advanced on horseback, threatened by shafts from all sides, and his trained mount trampled the fallen enemy. Was this not in some way a repetition of the vision at Grand, ever present in the minds of the emperor and his soldiers: the spectacle of this divine rider in a transport of glory, his face gleaming and transfigured by the glitter of precious stones which made his helmet glow with a supernatural light? . . .

Later, the labarum would be Christianized by a very simple and clever addition. A plot would be progressively fabricated, the chronological development of which the successive texts of Lactantius and Eusebius describe.

ANDRÉ PIGANIOL (1883–1968), late professor of Roman civilization in the Collège de France, wrote many books on a variety of Roman topics, including a first-rate survey of the fourth century A.D., *L'Empire Chrétien* (1947). In the following selection, from *L'Empereur Constantin* (1932), Piganiol argues that the "official" panegyrics delivered in 310, 311, 312, and 321 clearly indicate both the primacy of the pagan vision of 310 ("the only authentic vision of Constantine") and the development of Constantine's syncretic religious policy. Piganiol's Constantine is not the Machiavellian ruler depicted by Burckhardt or Grégoire, but a rather simple and superstitious child of the age.*

André Piganiol

# Neither Mystic nor Imposter

"Upon becoming emperor Constantine had nothing more urgent to do than to restore the Christians to their religion and their god," wrote Lactantius around 320. Constantine must have published an edict of toleration at the time of his accession in 306, or at least when he took the title of Augustus, in 307. Such was the official truth a few years after the battle of the Milvian Bridge.

Nothing confirms the accuracy of Lactantius' thesis, and, to tell the truth, he himself, who does not seem to have been called to Constantine's court before 317, merely repeated what he had been told at that time. From all appearances Constantine continued to follow the tolerant policy of his father. We notice that in the territory of Maximin Daia, in 308–309, the Christians enjoyed a brief respite, but still nothing warrants our saying that Constantine intervened on their behalf. Nor is there any valid reason to think that Spain's submission to Constantine was due to the influence of the Christians of that country.

We cannot even assert that Constantine adopted, from his accession, the celestial and solar monotheism of his father. It is true that he struck coins on which the emperor Constantius is seen ascending into the heavens and received by the sun [Sol]. But he was merely illustrating in this way the official theory of the imperial consecration. The sun-god appeared on coins of Augustus Severus (died in 308), of

*André Piganiol, *L'Empereur Constantin* (Paris: Rieder, 1932), pp. 48–75. Translated by John W. Eadie. Footnotes omitted.

Augustus Galerius, during a period when Constantine still seemed to prefer the image of the god Mars *(Mars pater propugnator)* [Father Mars Defender]. We may conjecture that during these first years Constantine came little by little under the influence of Constantius' advisers and favorites. It is only after this indoctrination that he appears as the heir of Constantius' religious thought. The names of the architects of this true conversion are not known.

Constantine's conversion to the solar cult was hastened by a sort of miracle of which we possess a detailed account. While he was leading his army south to put down the revolt of Maximian, the barbarians threatened the unguarded Rhine frontier. He sought the assistance of the gods and formulated solemn vows, if they should grant his prayer. After his victory over Maximian, as he was returning to the Rhine in all haste, he made a detour in order to visit the world-renowned temple of Apollo, perhaps that of Grand in the territory of the Leuci. Precisely then he learned that order had just been restored on the Rhine and that the time had come for him to fulfill his vows. In the temple of Apollo he had a vision: The god appeared, accompanied by Victory and holding out to him two laurel crowns, within each of which was a mysterious sign. He thought this sign foretold that he would one day celebrate the thirtieth anniversary of his reign (the feast of the *tricennalia*). Moreover, he recognized himself in the features of the god. He lavished unprecedented gifts upon the temple, and word of his munificence spread across Gaul. All the priests of Apollo begged him to visit their temples; they expected that as soon as peace was reestablished the emperor, a devout pilgrim, would make the rounds of the temples, dispensing offerings and privileges.

Already sanctuaries had sprung up in his footsteps.

This account describes the only authentic vision of Constantine. The legend of the vision of 312 is nothing but a Christian adaptation. The vision in the spring of 310 is described with the date, place, and circumstances in the panegyric delivered at Trèves in July 310, in the presence of the emperor himself. The anonymous orator who was its author received his information from Constantine personally, just as it is he who first mentioned publicly the titles which the emperor claimed to derive from his kinship with the family of Claudius II. We have here an account which dates from only a few months after the event it recounts and which emanated directly from the prince.

This curious episode reveals all the hidden motives which later led to Constantine's conversion to Christianity. He did not take up arms without invoking the gods; the magic sign he observed on an *ex voto* aroused his imagination; he readily lavished gifts upon the god and his priests. But Apollo benefited for some time from the extraordinary fortune that was soon to serve Jesus.

It would be very important to know precisely what magic signs were seen by Constantine at Grand. We already know that the number 30 was recognized there. Besides, coins struck between 317 and 320 in several mints in the West frequently depicted a crown on the front of an altar, and inside the crown either the tau cross T, the cross with equal branches, or a star. It is quite probable that the prototypes of these crowns and symbols were seen by Constantine in the Gallic temple of Apollo. The sign T (or perhaps the nearness of the two signs T and X, interpreted as *tria decennia*) must have been understood at the moment as indicating the promise of a thirtieth anniversary (the *tricennalia*). Constantine will never forget the strange emblems of the Celtic sanctuary, which he interpreted without any doubt as signifying the divine promise of a long reign.

Henceforth Constantine considered Sol as the founder of the Claudian dynasty, with which he claimed affiliation after Maximian's downfall. He is not the only emperor who struck coins in the name of Sol *(Soli invicto comiti)*, but he is the only one who had represented on his coins the effigy of Sol and himself, in two parallel profiles. This remarkable image appeared shortly after the Apollonian miracle, in 310. . . .

The panegyric delivered at Trèves in July 311 in Constantine's presence on the anniversary of his accession defines his religious thinking clearly. He did not intend to deprive polytheism of its honors: When he had returned to Autun, a short time before, "the statues of all the gods" were carried to meet him, and the faithful prayed for him in all the temples. But he had a particular devotion to Apollo: "If the emperor comes to Autun," says the orator, Sol will escort him, for he is "the companion and associate of his majesty." From the time of the vision at Grand, Constantine believed himself to be a kinsman of Sol. He did not, however, consider Sol as the supreme god, but rather as the visible symbol of "that divine spirit which governs the universe and whose designs are immediately realized."

Thus, without breaking with traditional paganism Constantine purified it and oriented it toward a cosmology suitable for reconciling religion and philosophy. . . . Constantine at this time reminds one of that other fascinating prince, Julian the Apostate, who also loved Gaul and defended it well. Both were tormented by religious preoccupations; both directed their thoughts to Sol and to hea-

ven. Only Constantine will be converted by bishops, while Julian will be deluded by charlatans. . . .

The war between Maxentius and Constantine was not a war of religion, in the sense that Constantine in no way set himself up as the avenger of persecuted Christians. But it was all the same a war of gods, in that each adversary had his divine auxiliaries. If, as is probable, Constantine was acquainted with Maxentius' magical observances, he certainly wanted to counter the fantastic allies of his enemy with other invisible allies. Before the battle, he had a magic sign inscribed on the shield of his soldiers, and it is to the efficacy of this sign that he attributed his victory.

Citing the testimony of Constantine himself, the ancients specify that he invoked the God of the Christians against the demons of Maxentius and that he conquered under the sign of the cross. Modern authorities subscribe rather willingly to this interpretation. If Constantine, they say, on the eve of a decisive battle raised a Christian sign over his army, this was because his affection was from this moment on won over to Christianity.

However, we immediately perceive a serious difficulty. The Constantinian sign was not the cross but a sort of star monogram, composed of an X-shaped cross intersected by a vertical staff whose top curved inward. The ancients ordinarily interpreted this sign as if it were composed of the first two letters X and P of the Greek name of Christ. It is certain that in inscriptions and papyri the sign ☧ was occasionally used long before Constantine as an abbreviation for Greek words beginning with *chr*. This is the form the Constantinian monogram later took and which is known to us from a great many specimens dispersed throughout the Empire. But we know other very ancient forms of the monogram, which cannot be interpreted as the conjunction of the two letters X and P. Around 317 the coins of Siscia depicted on Constantine's helmet, between two authentic monograms of the classic type, a curious symbol with an upright head ⚕. The aberrant and unintelligible forms are probably the primitive forms and the classic form an adaptation.

Constantine maintained that the sign painted on the shields had been revealed to him in a heavenly vision. The classification of evidence—thus Voltaire proceeded in the *Philosophical Dictionary*— enables us to follow the successive stages and the development of the legend.

It is impossible to deny the reality of the following fact: Constantine had a sign depicted on the soldiers' shields, and he attributed his victory to this sign. In fact, after his entry into Rome he had a statue erected, probably in the Forum, which represented him holding in his hand the magic emblem. Unfortunately Eusebius, who did not see it, is the only author who describes it, and in rather vague terms; at least this description is quite early, since it is found in the ninth book of the *Ecclesiastical History,* composed around 315. According to Eusebius, Constantine held "in his right hand" the "trophy of the salutary passion," the "sign of salvation." A Latin inscription, carved on the base of the statue, of which Eusebius doubtless gives us an approximate Greek translation, announced to the Romans that Constantine had triumphed by this salutary sign, the *emblem*—or more precisely the *proof—of courage.*

This statue is probably identical with the one set up by the Senate in honor of Constantine. But the panegyric of Constantine delivered at Trèves in 313 informs us that it depicted the emperor with the features of a god. What we know of Constantine's religious beliefs warrants our thinking that the statue represented Constantine-Apollo.

In the East, travelers spread the news that in Rome, in the Forum, was a statue of Constantine holding the sign of the cross, and that the base of the monument had an inscription to the glory of Christ. Eusebius was probably alluding to this statue when, in the discourse delivered at the dedication of the church of Tyre (about 314), he announced that the emperors, in the heart of Rome, had proclaimed the great deeds of Christ and the victories he won over the godless.

If we dismiss the Christian interpretation, the facts amount to this: Shortly after the battle of the Milvian Bridge, a statue was set up in Rome of Constantine-Apollo, holding "in his hand" a magic sign, to which the emperor attributed the power to bestow victory and to which he owed his own. Besides this sign, the emperor probably held in his other hand the cruciform staff of a trophy.

The earliest account we have of the campaign of 312 is provided by the orator who delivered the panegyric of Trèves, no doubt in the presence of the emperor, in July 313. This panegyric, like the other texts in this series, was certainly an officially inspired document and employed for propaganda. If we compare it with the panegyrics of 310 and 311, it is clear that the religious thought of the emperor had widened. There is no allusion to Apollo. The supreme deity delegates to the inferior gods *(dii minores)* the responsibility of looking after common men, but he communicates directly with Constantine and "deigns to reveal himself to him." The allusion to a vision appears here to be unquestionable. Who is this supreme deity *(quisnam te deus. . . .)?* The orator calls upon the "creator of the world" *(summe rerum sator),* who has as many names as there are languages among men, and who may be conceived of, either as an intellect *(mens divina)* which, according to the Stoic conception, penetrates the elements of the entire world, or as a power seated above the vault of heaven *(supra omne caelum)* and contemplating his work from afar. Thus Constantine wished his victory to be attributed to divine inspiration; he even boasted that he had countered the admonitions of the haruspices, who had advised against combat, with precepts he had received directly from the Supreme Deity. This God is described in rather vague terms so that Christians as well as enlightened pagans might be able to recognize in him the customary object of their worship.

In 314, a small cross with equal branches appeared on coins struck in the mint at Tarragona. But this sign was engraved on pieces that bore the image of Sol and the dedication *Soli invicto comiti.* This was merely a "different," moneyer, a mint mark which reveals the presence of Christian workers in the corps of moneyers at Tarragona.

In 315, the inscription on the triumphal arch dedicated in Rome in honor of Constantine proclaimed that he had conquered, a very vague formula: "by divine inspiration" *(instinctu divinitatis).*

Around the same year, Eusebius revised book nine of his *Ecclesiastical History* and recounted there the victory of the Milvian Bridge. It is here that he describes the statue of Constantine holding the sign of the cross. He states that Constantine had invoked the Christian God and that he owed his victory to Him. But this is probably only a hypothesis to explain the extraordinary statue. Eusebius mentions neither a vision nor a sign depicted on the shields.

It is on coins struck by the mint of Siscia, between 317 and 320, that the classic monogram ☧ appeared for the first time

on Constantine's helmet alongside the monogram of aberrant form ☼. We cannot confirm that the classic monogram was added as early as this to the standard which bore the laureate effigies of the emperor and the imperial princes, and to which the language of the soldiers, through distortion, gave the common name of *labarum.*

A little later, in Lactantius' pamphlet *On the Death of the Persecutors,* which we are inclined to date from 320, we encounter the first draft of the definitive version. Before the battle, Constantine was advised while sleeping *(in quiete)* to mark on the shields a divine emblem *(caeleste signum dei),* composed of the Greek letter X intersected by a vertical staff, whose head was bent *(transversa X littera, summo capite circumflexo);* and this emblem designated Christ. It is not certain whether Lactantius then had before his eyes the classic monogram rather than an aberrant form; and from the details he gives it seems that the interpretation of the monogram was not evident to the Christians themselves.

The panegyric delivered in the presence of Constantine by the orator Nazarius in March 321 enables us to understand other embellishments to the legend. It was reported in Gaul that heavenly squadrons had been seen, who said that they had been sent by the deity to aid Constantine against Maxentius. Their arms shone with a strange glow, and they kept repeating: "It is Constantine whom we seek."

The classic image of the labarum surmounted by a Constantinian monogram appeared for the first time after 326 on coins from Constantinople.

Finally, after Constantine's death, Eusebius gave the definitive version: He received it from the lips of the emperor himself, who vouched for its truth under oath. Shortly after noon, as the day was already fading, Constantine saw above the disc of the sun the trophy of the cross and the inscription, "Conquer by this sign." Soldiers were present and verified the prodigy. Then the following night Christ appeared to him, showed him the same sign, and directed him to have it reproduced. Constantine sent for the goldsmiths. Sitting among them, he instructed them to execute an insignia, which Eusebius describes and which is none other than the labarum. Finally Constantine sought the opinion of the priests, who explained to him that the god of his vision was Christ and that the cross was the trophy of Christ's victory over death in times past.

While Lactantius dates the vision to the eve of the battle, Eusebius says that Constantine experienced it in Gaul before beginning the campaign against Maxentius.

In 351, the inhabitants of Jerusalem witnessed an analogous miracle. A luminous cross appeared in the sky above Golgotha, and remained visible for several hours. The bishop Cyril informed the emperor Constantius of this miracle which was more remarkable, according to him, than even the discovery of the wood of the cross in the time of the emperor Constantine. One is surprised at Cyril's silence regarding the cross which, according to Eusebius, had appeared in the sky before Constantine himself. But in 351 the situation was different: The extraordinary and unprecedented miracle was the appearance of a cross above the place of the Passion; nothing like this had happened in the time of Constantine.

Furthermore, many readers consider Eusebius' account pure fiction. We know through Gelasius (1, 5)[1] the arguments by which its authenticity was defended: the miracle of 351, attested by witnesses was used; moreover, it was recalled, accounts of equally incredible marvels were to be found in the Old Testament, in the history of Alexander, and in the Greek poets; Jews and pagans were therefore ill advised to challenge the reality of the Constantinian miracle.

Actually the legend triumphed, and at the beginning of the fifth century Philostorgius[2] even embellished it further. According to him, Constantine had seen the sign of the cross in the sky surrounded by stars whose position formed a Latin inscription. Some aberrant traditions persisted. According to one, Constantine had had his vision in the course of a campaign against the barbarians of the Danube.

After having followed the steps in the formation of the legend, we can perhaps discern the historical elements in it.

There is only one authentic vision of Constantine, that which he had in Gaul in a temple of Apollo. It is in Gaul that Eusebius' last account places the scene of the miracle, and according to the author the sign seen by Constantine was closely linked to the sun. After 310 Constantine was constantly obsessed by the memory of the symbols he had seen in the Gallic temple in the hands of a solar god who resembled him like a brother.

These are the magic signs he had painted on the shields on the eve of the battle in order to counter Maxentius' magic. It was to their efficacy that he attributed his victory, and these are the emblems he had depicted in the hands of the statue, which probably represented him in Rome in the precise pose of the god who appeared to him in Gaul.

---

[1] Gelasius of Cyzicus (flor. 5th century). — Ed.

[2] Philostorgius, an Arian philosopher (ca. 364–425). — Ed.

What were these divine emblems? Probably the two cruciform signs: the cross with equal branches and the tau cross T which appears on Constantinian coins. Had he thought to fuse them into a star-shaped symbol ⚹? In this way a sign is obtained which could easily lend itself to the divergent interpretations which have been put forward.

It is clear that the Constantinian symbol puzzled the Christians themselves. Eusebius and Lactantius describe it as an unprecedented sign which they can compare to nothing else. Eusebius believed that a cross, the trophy of the Saviour's passion, could be recognized in it. Later, the intersection of the first two letters of the name of Christ were discerned in it. A work of stylization gave to the fantastic sign a definitive Christian form.

"Having left Gaul a pagan, Constantine arrived in Rome a Christian," writes one of the greatest experts on the Constantine period. Let us not say that in 312 Constantine became a Christian; let us say that he had been won over to the cult of the cross. The Christians had provided him with the decisive explanation of these magic signs that had intrigued him for months. He marked the cross on his forehead, as the Christians did. He raised crosses throughout his empire.

Constantine had thought that he had conquered in the name of Sol. The priests, seeing the symbol which was dear to him, exclaimed that he had conquered in the name of Christ. Constantine believed it. He was a Christian without knowing it. In order to be a Christian, it seems, he did not even need to repudiate the solar cult, since the symbols were the same. . . .

Constantine was neither a mystic nor an imposter, but a sincere individual who sought the truth — on the threshold of a mysterious century when human reason faltered — a poor man groping his way.

Lactantius' account of the conversion is the focus of the following selection by JACQUES MOREAU (1918–1961), late professor of ancient history in the University of the Saar, who also edited Lactantius' pamphlet *On the Deaths of the Persecutors* (1954). His general appraisal of Lactantius' testimony raises once again the fundamental question: To what extent can we trust the literary accounts of the conversion?*

Jacques Moreau

# Syncretic Propaganda

Immediately after the "conversion" of Constantine, . . . it was very difficult to present the victory he had won as a victory of the cross or christogram, signs revealed to the emperor by divine intervention. Accordingly, one finds no trace of these σημεῖα [signs] in Eusebius' account, either in the edition of 315 of the *Ecclesiastical History* or in the last version, completed after 326, on which the Syriac translation is based.

At most the well-informed historian mentions that the statue of Constantine, erected by order of the Senate in commemoration of the victory of the Milvian Bridge, held in the right hand the salutary sign, σωτήριον σημεῖον.

Lactantius, on the other hand, in chapter XLIV of his *On the Deaths of the Persecutors*, attributes the crushing and unexpected defeat of the forces of Maxentius to the effect of the *caeleste signum dei* [heavenly sign of God] with which Constantine, admonished in a dream, had adorned the shields of his soldiers.

How does one explain this divergence? It is that Lactantius, writing around 318–320, at a time when neither of the emperors had an antichristian policy, did not wish to favor Licinius to the detriment of Constantine. In 313 Licinius had defeated Maximin Daia, an authentic persecutor, in a battle fought under the protection of the Christian god. Hoping to win favor with the eastern provinces, where Christians were particularly numerous, he

---

*Jacques Moreau, "Sur la Vision de Constantin," *Revue des Études Anciennes,* 55 (1953), 307–333. Translated by John W. Eadie. Footnotes omitted.

quite naturally posed as a defender of the Christian cause assailed by successive Augusti of Nicomedia.

In the battle of Campus Ergenus [April 30, 313] the prayer which he had his soldiers recite had persuaded the Christians, who were numerous in the army of Daia, not to resist those who beseeched, or seemed to beseech, their God, and thus he had accomplished the defeat of the emperor-persecutor.

The Christians had attributed to the miraculous intervention of an angel the strategem which had assured victory to Licinius. From this time on, in order not to weaken Constantine's position with respect to his colleague, it was essential that he should have received from heaven a favor comparable to that which Licinius had enjoyed and that his victory should have been a Christian victory of the same type as that of Campus Ergenus. This is why Lactantius, echoing the Christian contingent in the court, describes a dream of Constantine analogous to Licinius' dream and attributes his master's victory to the miraculous performance of a Christian *signum,* just as Licinius had owed his success to a prayer disclosed in a supernatural way.

It is quite different with Eusebius. In the first version of book nine of the *Ecclesiastical History* the stress is placed exclusively on eastern affairs, and Licinius appears in it as the instrument of God, while Constantine's part is very modest. In the first revision of this text the two emperors are treated with equal sympathy, but Licinius retains the principal role; the victory at the Milvian Bridge is mentioned only briefly. The last revision, after the final defeat of Licinius, is a great deal more "Constantinian"; the battle for Rome takes on much greater importance, while Licinius' actions are reduced to a minimum compatible with historical

reality. If, between 315 and around 320, Constantine needed to make known in the East, whose sympathies he sought, a Christian version of the deeds which presented him as at least the equal of Licinius in 313, champion of the new religion, it is no less evident that for his part Licinius had no interest at all in popularizing an account of the vision at Rome which served the propaganda of his rival. It is therefore natural that Eusebius had had no knowledge of the prodigy of the Milvian Bridge. In the version of the *Ecclesiastical History* revised after the definitive victory of Constantine, the episode no longer has a place. It had become useless to balance the past merits of Licinius with those of his adversary, the Campus Ergenus with the Milvian Bridge. Eventually Licinius' prayer would be transferred purely and simply to Constantine's account; the simple dream reported by Lactantius would become the vision of a celestial cross and, by a considerable anachronism, that vision would be the origin of this labarum whose existence was scarcely conceivable before the decisive campaign of 324.

There was then no longer any question of comparing the merits of the two Christian or Christianophile emperors. The Church had triumphed and history could be rewritten; the important thing was to give the earliest possible date for Constantine's conversion and to depict him enjoying abundant divine favor from the very outset of his career, at the time of the first great war which he had conducted. Lactantius, on the other hand, wrote at a time when the die was not yet cast. The Christians favored Licinius as much as Constantine, and the latter's one concern was not to allow himself to be outstripped by his rival. We know that after 310 Constantine no longer endeavored to legitimize his pretensions to the Empire, by his affiliation with the Herculian dynasty, which had been discredited by the conspiracy of Maximian and the usurpation of Maxentius, but by his "adoption of Sol-Apollo as divine protector, or more precisely, by his wish to identify himself with him," and by the fiction of the Claudian origin of the Second Flavians, a means of propaganda moreover inherited from Constantius. The cult of Sol was the most suitable for bringing together on the religious level all pagan subjects of the Empire and offered besides the inestimable advantage of not destroying the bridges between its devotees and the Christians, whom Constantine had always taken care to treat with leniency. The comparison of Sol and the Redeemer, "Light of the World," "Star of Salvation," was so familiar to the faithful of the first centuries that numerous pagans could believe that the "Sun of Justice" was the God of Christians. In addition to which Constantine's Christianity blended curiously with the cult of Light and the cult of the Sun.

The solar religion adopted by Constantine from 310 on was in no way offensive to Christians, especially as it evolved rapidly toward the cult of an unnamed divinity, the Sun being only a sort of demiurge, an intermediary between the created universe and the Creator, whose visible emanation he was.

On this point, then, there was no difficulty to be feared, and the emperor, one must suppose, had too much interest in remaining on good terms with the Christians to put an end to an ambiguity which satisfied at one stroke both Christians and enlightened pagans.

But precisely the ambiguity of the imperial theology must have been used to advantage both by the Christians of the court and by their adversaries, each side endeavoring to present the action and conduct of the prince in a manner favorable to its cause and at the same time attempting, even if at the cost of a scarcely orthodox interpretation, to bring the emperor himself to sanction such and such a version. Will we not see Lactantius in the *Divine Institutions,* dedicated to Constantine, declaring that contemplation of the sun bestows the idea of God, and the clerks of the court working out for the emperor's use a curious doctrine uniting the teachings of the Church, the doctrine of Plato's *Timaeus,* and the reveries of Vergil.

It was consequently easy enough for the Christians in Constantine's entourage—from at least 313 it included the bishop Ossius; and Lactantius arrived at the court in 317 at the latest—to present in a Christian light any attitude whatsoever of the prince and to reply to pagan propaganda put forward concerning certain conduct by means of a different interpretation.

It is in this way, we believe, that the vision reported by Lactantius must be interpreted. Licinius had received a direct revelation from on high; it was necessary that Constantine too should be found to be in communication with God. Apollo had appeared to Constantine in 310; it was necessary that this prince also receive the favor of a Christian vision. The dream at the Milvian Bridge was a reply to both the pagan vision in the Gallic sanctuary and the advice given to Licinius by an angel.

This is why it is useless to search for any historical reality in Lactantius' account: a vision related by the emperor to his intimates; a dream interpreted by his counselors, etc. What Lactantius describes, the "sign" which, according to him, adorned the shields of Constantine's soldiers, is the monogram of Christ which began to appear on coins from 317; he projects into the past creation of the sign under which his master hoped to rally the eastern

Christians to his cause, although it was of quite recent origin at the time when he wrote. Thus he gave legitimacy to a mode of propaganda which Constantine intended to use as ideological preparation for the war of 324.

But must we conclude that Lactantius' informants invented, along with the dream, the sign revealed to Constantine? Had not some event occurred around 312 which might in some way verify the account in *On the Deaths?* In an epoch-making article H. Grégoire put forward the hypothesis that the sign inscribed on the soldiers' shields was none other than the X of the *vota,* which differed only by an iota from the said preconstantinian Christian monogram ✳. This *vota* sign had a magic significance, which it owed to "the only officially certified vision of Constantine, which was commended to the belief of the masses by an authentic prayer . . . , the pagan vision of 310."

One cannot examine separately the pagan vision of 310 and the Christian dream of 312. It must be observed, nonetheless, that Lactantius' account in no way seems to be an adaptation of the episode in the Gallic temple. There, Apollo appeared to Constantine in person. The god was accompanied by Victory and bore laurel crowns, each of which presaged a reign of thirty years. And the panegyrist exclaimed, "This is the duration which is fixed for your existence, which will exceed that of the old man of Pylos."

There is question here of an omen of a long and happy reign, not of the granting of a magic sign destined to guarantee victory. Moreover, the dream recounted by Lactantius in a manner so dry and terse, appears tame indeed compared with the manifestation of Apollo, who treated Constantine almost as an equal. It does not seem, then, that the episode of the Milvian Bridge constitutes a Christian trans-

position of the Gallic vision. Lactantius would in this case have made the triumphal apparition of 310 insipid to the point of rendering it unrecognizable.

As to the account in the panegyric of 310, it is perhaps not as original as has been suggested. It could well be a simple amplification of an episode in the life of Aurelian. We know that, according to the *Historia Augusta,*[1] Apollonius appeared to this emperor while he was planning to destroy Tyana. The philosopher, anxious to save his native city, advised him to refrain from spilling innocent blood if he wished to conquer, to rule, and to live. Given the late date and the tendentious character of the *Historia Augusta,* G. Costa believed he could conclude that the appearance of Apollonius of Tyana to Aurelian was an antichristian version of the vision of Constantine at the Milvian Bridge. The prestige of Aurelian and of his tutelary deity Sol should have counterbalanced Constantine's glory, which was attained with the help of the Christian God. The pagan tone and the polemical bent of the *Life of Aurelian* are undeniable, but it does not follow that it has borrowed the essential features of the vision from the legendary story of Constantine in order to combat it. Indeed, if Costa were able to compare certain expressions in the *Life* with analogous expressions in the Constantinian period [he would find that] it is always a question of texts which do not have any Christian character: the panegyric of 321 and the inscription on the triumphal arch of 315.

It is in fact the story of Aurelian, known at the time of Lactantius and of the panegyrists through accounts used later in the *Annales* of Virius Nicomachus Flavianus,[2]

---

[1] The *Augustan History* is a series of biographies of the emperors from Hadrian to Diocletian.—Ed.

[2] A high-ranking pagan aristocrat (flor. late fourth century).—Ed.

which served as model for the pagan vision of 310 and for the miraculous episode, also entirely of pagan inspiration, referred to by Nazarius in 321.

Constantine, dreaming of unifying the empire, of necessity drew inspiration from the example of Aurelian, the great *restitutor orbis Romani* [restorer of the Roman world]. The moment was opportune for the pagans in his entourage, won over to the idea of a purified and universal religion, to attempt to win over the prince entirely by pointing out that he was following in the footsteps of a great precursor and that the supreme god was showing a greater favor to him than he had to Aurelian. Thus the *omen tricenum* [the thirty-year omen] of the Gallic Apollo appears to be an exaggeration of the conditional prediction of Apollonius of Tyana: "to conquer, to rule, to live."

But if the Gallic vision was not the prototype of the dream of the Milvian Bridge—which was itself merely an adaptation of Licinius' dream and doubtless aimed at causing it to be forgotten—it does not necessarily follow that the sign of 312 was not inspired by a presumed sign of 310.

The panegyrist does not speak of signs, omens of a reign of thirty years which were encircled by the crowns of Apollo and Victory. But this *omen* could scarcely be represented except by the number X repeated three times: The god brought the prince *signa* similar to those seen on crowns offered to emperors on their twentieth anniversary in office and which were the customary *vota*, SIC XX SIC XXX. At first glance Grégoire's hypothesis is attractive: the X of the Gallic temple differs only by an iota from the sign on the shields. This identification, however, poses certain difficulties. If the representation of Victory inscribing the numbers of *vota* on a shield is a common theme of imperial coinage, and especially of Constantinian coinage, nothing certifies in return that the soldiers' arms ever bore such signs.

As the sign described by Lactantius is not a modification of that of the *vota*, must one conclude that it was a Christian sign and that consequently the conversion of Constantine was, in 311, an accomplished fact?

This view, with slight variations, was accepted almost unanimously up to the time when Grégoire's famous article forced historians to reconsider the question. Even today many scholars, and not the least important, continue to believe that the sign on the shields was really a Christian sign. One of the most eminent of these, A. Alföldi, asserts that the emperor, after the revelation with which we are acquainted and guided more by a superstitious feeling than deep conviction, had his troops fight under the protection of the monogram of Christ, an emblem whose precise character most people did not know. For his part, A. M. Groag conjectures that Constantine, in displaying Christian views with every possible ostentation, wished to win over the numerous Christian soldiers, Romans and Africans, in Maxentius' army. To Groag one may reply that such a stratagem had to succeed, and it did in fact when it was a question of combatting a declared enemy of the Christian religion: the prayer of Licinius' soldiers led a great part of Daia's army to desert on the battlefield. But why would Christians in Maxentius' army leave, for religious reasons, the camp of a ruler who had furnished so many proofs of his good will toward the Church? For this, Constantine would have had to have been considered a convinced Christian, for some time before the battle, and no one would think of maintaining this.

Alföldi's hypothesis can be opposed with some weighty arguments. First, in order to secure his position, he gives 313 as the date of composition of *On the Deaths,* with the addition of two chapters in 315. The account of the battle of the Milvian Bridge would then represent the version current in the emperor's entourage and the opinion of the latter and his court, just as it was immediately issued from the event, before political-religious propaganda could take over the story and present it in a tendentious manner. On the contrary, Lactantius' pamphlet completed around 318–320, at a time of growing tension, as yet muffled, between Licinius and Constantine is already a story transformed with a view to winning over the Christians of the East to Constantine's cause. In these circumstances it is necessary to subject the author's statements to close scrutiny, particularly, those which deal with the religious policy of the two emperors.

Besides, if Constantine in 312 adopted, consciously or not, a Christian emblem, how are we to explain the total absence of similar embellishment not only on the monuments sponsored by the Senate, which would be understandable, but also on the coins of the period? How are we to account for the fact that neither the panegyric of 313 nor that of 321 says a word about it; how are we to interpret the gold medallion, struck on the very day after the capture of Rome, on which the emperor's effigy is juxtaposed to the twin representation of the solar deity?

One could consider that the year 312 marked a turning point in Constantine's policy; one could emphasize the unexpected changes from 311 on in the language of the panegyrists, who no longer mention pagan deities by name. But, as Orgels has clearly seen, this is a question of an attempted reconciliation of traditional polytheism and philosophical monotheism, not of an echo of an alleged renunciation by the emperor of all former errors. To convince oneself of this it suffices to compare the above-mentioned panegyrics with the curious passage inserted in the *Corpus Hermeticum*[3] which, in a verbose style, praises the Tetrarchs by glorifying Almighty God, supreme monarch of the universe, and which certainly is not suspected of latent or manifest Christianity. And even the terms by which Constantine, from 313, testifies to his sympathy for the Christian religion—"the cult in which the highest reverence of the most holy and heavenly Providence is maintained"—are too visibly inspired by "philosophical" phraseology to bear witness to a complete transformation. This explains in addition why the inscription on the Arch of Constantine mentions only the anonymous "divinity," while Sol is everywhere present in the decoration of the monument, and why this same deity, whose name the panegyrists do not utter, continues to reign on Constantine's coinage down to the eve of the second war with Licinius. That Constantine had a less reserved attitude toward the Christians after Ossius appeared on the scene should not surprise us, but one cannot infer from this change evidence which proves [that there was] a conversion.

---

[3] A collection of occult writings (first to third centuries A.D.) attributed to Hermes Tresmegistos = the Egyptian god Thoth.—Ed.

NORMAN H. BAYNES (1877–1961), barrister and
distinguished Byzantine scholar, is one of the ablest
defenders of the genuineness and sincerity of
Constantine's conversion. In his Raleigh Lecture of
1929 delivered before the British Academy, Baynes
examines "Constantine's own letters and edicts" (many
of which are reproduced in translation) and concludes
not only that Constantine accepted Christianity in 312,
but also that the principal goal of his administration
was the achievement of unity within the Catholic
Church.*

Norman H. Baynes

# Religiosissimus Augustus

To take man's past and demonstrate its
inherent logic is a fascinating pursuit—
to prove to one's own satisfaction that the
past could not have been otherwise than it
was, being a necessary development from
that which had gone before, this is gratify-
ing to man, for he can thus look back upon
human history and regard it as in a sense
his own creation and can then praise its
creator. In this reconstruction of the past,
however, difficulties are at times caused
by the interposition in the stream of history of outstanding personalities which
resist rationalization and remain unexpected and embarrassing. One of these
personalities is Constantine the Great. To
my mind, at least, all attempts to explain
away Constantine as the natural outcome
of the previous history of Rome have
failed completely. Constantine can only
be satisfactorily interpreted in terms of
the Zeitgeist [spirit of the age] if the Zeitgeist is arbitrarily fashioned in the likeness of Constantine. The more closely
Constantine's life and achievement are
studied, the more inevitably is one driven
to see in them an erratic block which has
diverted the stream of human history. It
may be true that by A.D. 311 the imperial
policy of persecution of the Christians
had been proved a failure—Galerius, the
instigator of that policy, had publicly confessed its futility—but this failure could
not carry with it the implication that it
was the duty of a Roman Emperor so far
to disavow Rome's past as himself to adopt

*"Constantine the Great and the Christian Church," by Norman H. Baynes, from *Proceedings of the
British Academy,* vol. XV, 1929, 341–360, 367–368, published by the Oxford University Press for the British
Academy. Footnotes omitted.

the faith professed by perhaps one-tenth of his subjects. Constantine presents to the student of history so interesting a problem precisely because he is an intractable individual, because he was not merely the creation of the past, but marked in himself a new beginning which was in such large measure to determine the future of the Roman world.

The representations attempted by modern scholars of the convictions and aims of Constantine have been so diverse that at times it is hard to believe that it is one and the same emperor that they are seeking to portray. As students of history we protest energetically that a man can only be rightly understood if he be regarded against the background of his world, that he can only be fairly judged in the light of the standards and the values of the society in which he lived; and then, having formulated the principle, we straightway forget it. We write our biographies in terms of the thought of our own day and impose upon another age the standards with which we are familiar. Burckhardt began his famous chapter upon Constantine and the Christian Church with the remark: "In the case of a man of genius, whose ambition and love of power refuse to him a moment's peace, there can be no question of Christianity or paganism, of conscious religion or irreligion. Such a man even when he persuades himself that he has his place in an ecclesiastical community is essentially *un*religious." The issue is thus, you observe, pre-judged, and the answer to the problem cannot be for an instant in doubt. Eusebius wrote a work which, had he been publishing it to-day, he would probably have entitled, "Constantine and the Christian religion: a contribution towards imperial biography." After Burckhardt's opening sentence we may be sure that Eusebius will receive short shrift, and we are not disappointed. For the ra-

tionalist of the mid-nineteenth century there can be no hesitation: Constantine's supreme misfortune has been that the unhappy emperor fell into the hands of the most repulsive of all panegyrists who has falsified the portrait "durch und durch" [thoroughly]. "Eusebius is the first historian of antiquity who was *durch und durch* dishonest." But we may well ask: was any Roman of the fourth century "essentially *un*religious"? "In this age there were no such persons as free-thinkers," says M. Lot, and he is probably not far from the truth.

Or again, consider Otto Seeck as he discusses the authenticity of documents attributed by Eusebius to Constantine: the belief that the divine will had punished those emperors who had persecuted the Christians and preserved those who had not enforced the edicts of persecution is, he notes, common to Lactantius, Eusebius, and the documents purporting to represent the thought of Constantine; the idea was in many men's minds. "Why then should we be surprised if the good Constantine in his turn repeats the same trivialities?" Trivialities? But what if a man really believes that God does actively, consistently, intervene in human affairs, that victory and defeat, prosperity and adversity are alike in His gift?—and what if that man is the ruler of the Roman world? Is that belief then insignificant? is it not rather of supreme moment? So hard it is to think ourselves back into a world which is not our own!

And there remains a yet subtler danger: we may imagine that we have discovered the key to a personality, and then we persuade ourselves that it will open every lock. And yet it is surely but rarely that every secret door of thought and motive in human life will yield to a single master-key. Life is not so simple as that. Eduard Schwartz has done as much as any scholar in our day to advance the study of the reign of Constantine; in his book, *The Emperor Constantine and the Christian Church,* he has found the Open Sesame to the understanding of the reign in Constantine's resolution to exploit in his own interest the organization which gave to the Christian Church its corporate strength: through alliance with the Church Constantine sought to attain victory and the sole mastery of the Roman world. The emperor's toleration sprang from his desire that pagan and Christian alike should be conscious that they depended upon him alone. "Never," writes Schwartz, "has an emperor so triumphed over the Church as did Constantine in and through the Council of Nicaea;" the victory lay with the emperor's "diabolical cleverness." The one man who opposed Constantine was Athanasius, and in that contest of will Greek met Greek; for the opposition of Athanasius was inspired not by zeal for the true faith, not by any passion for the independence of the Church, but by the pride of a hierarch in the authority of his patriarchate. The masterkey in this analysis which Schwartz has given us of the personalities of Constantine and Athanasius is thus "Der Wille zur Macht" [the will to power]. But it may be doubted whether so extreme a simplification can do justice to the complexity of human convictions and human motives. The solution would appear rather to be imposed upon the evidence than to arise from a patient study of the documents themselves.

For myself, I have gradually come to the conviction that the true starting-point for any comprehension of the reign must be Constantine's own letters and edicts. That conclusion seems obvious enough, but so far as I am aware no one has yet consistently attempted from the evidence of these documents to sketch the aims and the thought of Constantine. Indeed the student is met by the initial difficulty of determining which of these documents are genuine and which are simply forgeries, whether contemporary forgeries of Eusebius, of Athanasius, of Christians in the imperial chancery, or later forgeries from the reign of Constantius, from the time of Valentinian, or even from the hand of fifth-century interpolators. My own view, which naturally you will not expect me to justify here, is that all the documents ascribed to Constantine in our sources are geniune, save only for a doubt in respect of the sermon addressed *To the Assembly of the Saints.* In the Greek version of that sermon, which alone has been preserved to us, I find it difficult to believe that we have a faithful translation of the Latin original as delivered by Constantine. I have therefore excluded it from . . . consideration. . . . So far as is possible, I have tried to avoid prepossessions; I desire that these documents may speak for themselves; from them let us try to outline the relations of Constantine towards the Christian Church.

A few words will suffice to rough in the background. In A.D. 293 Diocletian made Constantine's father, Constantius Chlorus, Caesar; he became the colleague of the western Augustus, Maximianus Herculius, the earthly representative of the divine Hercules. It was Constantius Chlorus who brought back Britain to the Roman allegiance after the overthrow of Carausius. Constantine himself did not remain with his father in the West, but lived at the court of Diocletian in Nicomedia or served his apprenticeship in arms under the Caesar Galerius. He was thus present in the East when in 303 Galerius forced upon Diocletian the policy of persecution. In 305 Diocletian left to Galerius the task of carrying on the bloody repression of Christianity which the Caesar had initiated, and together with Diocletian the western Augustus, Maximian, also abdicated. In the West, Constantius Chlorus became Augustus with Galerius for his eastern colleague. Constantine, summoned to Britain by his father, was acclaimed emperor by the army on the death of Constantius: he becomes a sovereign of the Herculian dynasty. The deities to whom he owes special devotion are thus Jupiter, the divine protector of the Jovian dynasty founded by Diocletian, and Hercules. When Maximian had reassumed the purple, becoming for a second time Augustus, and had given his daughter Fausta in marriage to Constantine, the association with the Herculian dynasty was rendered yet more intimate. But Maximian, seeking to remove Constantine, met his death; the Herculian line was discredited, and Constantine sought a new title for his sovereignty. He discovered that he was descended from Claudius II, the emperor who in the third century had stayed the Gothic invasion of the empire. The new title to rule carried with it a religious conversion: Constantine acknowledges as his divine protector the god whom his own family had worshipped—the Sun. In an age of religious syncretism this cult of the Sun adopted by the ruler of the Gallic provinces derives from many sources. Behind it lies the sun-worship of the Danubian provinces whence Constantine's family had migrated to the West; behind it lies the sun-worship of Zoroastrian Persia, and Aurelian's cult of the Unconquered Sun brought back from his eastern campaigns; while it was readily associated with the wide-spread Gallic worship of Apollo as god of light and healing and of sacred spring. And since this worship had been ancestral in Constantine's house, the Sun stands as symbol of the dynasty, the Claudian dynasty of the Second Flavians. Con-

stantius had refused in the West to execute the bloody edicts; under Constantine the West continued to enjoy religious peace. In 311 Galerius abandoned the policy of persecution: he capitulated, published his edict of toleration, and implored the prayers of the persecuted. That appeal was of no avail: a fortnight later he was dead, and Licinius was emperor in his place. In the West, Maxentius the son of Maximian held Italy, and on his father's death broke with Constantine and concluded an alliance with the eastern Caesar Maximin. It was a moment of crisis for Constantine: his forces were outnumbered by those of Maxentius; the latter had collected huge supplies of corn from Africa, and these were stored within the granaries of Rome; the newly-built walls of Aurelian made the western capital impregnable; two armies which had previously marched into Italy against Maxentius had perished miserably. In Rome Maxentius was supported by pagan prophets and augurs who promised victory, and in an age when it was really believed that victory or defeat was in the gift of Heaven, the sure promise of victory meant much: it was indeed by no means the "triviality" which it may appear to a modern rationalist. . . .

The gods of Rome, then, had declared for Maxentius; whence in this crisis should Constantine seek aid? Years later the emperor affirmed to Eusebius that he had seen a vision of the cross athwart the sun, and, beneath, the words, "In this conquer." Where Constantine was at this time, Eusebius does not tell us; a late legendary account says at Arles. That account has in itself no historical value, but it is at least *ben trovato* [well founded]. That is all the historian can say: "Eusebius asserts that Constantine affirmed to him" . . . but yet it is not quite all; he can add that against the advice of his general, against the counsel of the augurs, with amazing daring Constantine invaded Italy, and having defeated in the north of the peninsula the troops of Maxentius, took the still more surprising step of marching directly against the fortifications of the western capital. To my mind, I confess, this is more explicable if Constantine was convinced that the Christian God has assured him victory. Whether that appearance of the cross of light was only a subjective experience or whether it was an objective reality the historian cannot decide. Still less can he determine whether it was a God-granted miracle; to answer such a question the historian must turn philosopher or theologian; as historian he is perforce silent. He is unable to affirm miracle, but most certainly he cannot deny it. Just as is the case with Paul on the road to Damascus, so with Constantine in his hour of crisis the historian can but discuss the value of his sources and state the result of his criticism. Eusebius asserts that Constantine affirmed . . . For our purpose we may leave it at that. . . .

And before the walls of Rome a vision came to Constantine bidding him place upon the shields of his soldiers the Christian monogram. That command was obeyed, and the Sybilline books foretelling the defeat of the enemy of Rome drove Maxentius from the shelter of the walls of Aurelian to disaster and to death on the banks of the Tiber. The God of the Christians had kept His word. Constantine, as the inscription of the triumphal arch testifies, had saved the Roman state from the tyrant and his faction *instinctu divinitatis, mentis magnitudine*. There may be ambiguity in those words, but I would still translate them "by the prompting of the divinity, by the emperor's own greatness of mind"; they are contrasted, not parallel phrases.

Constantine, hailed as senior Augustus

by the senate, forthwith used his authority to dispatch to Maximin an order to stay the persecution and to issue a new decree of toleration. It is probable that at the same time—still in A.D. 312—he wrote to Anullinus, pro-consul in Africa, ordering him to restore to the churches all property which had formerly belonged to the Catholic Church in whosesoever hands that property—"gardens, houses or anything else"—might now be; while he informed Caecilianus, the Catholic bishop of Carthage, that instructions had been sent to the imperial *rationalis* in Africa to provide funds for distribution amongst the Catholics of Africa, Numidia, and Mauretania. Constantine, I would suggest, wrote these letters from Rome; already he knows of the Donatist schism in Africa and condemns it as a vain and bastard delusion (φαύλη ὑπονόθευσις). A little later, but before April 313, he gives orders to Anullinus that the Catholic clergy shall be freed from all public liturgies *(munera civilia)*. The interest of this letter lies in the reason given for the granting of this privilege—remember that Constantine is writing not to a Christian bishop, but to an imperial governor. "Since it appears from many considerations that through the setting at nought of the ritual (θρησκεία) in which the chief reverence for the most holy heavenly (power) is preserved great dangers have been brought upon the state, but when that ritual has been regularly resumed and is observed, there has resulted the greatest good fortune to the Roman name and remarkable prosperity in all human affairs, the divine beneficence granting this," therefore those who devote their lives to this service should have their reward. Already in Constantine's thought the Catholic priests through their priesthood are maintaining the fortunes of Rome. This is more than mere tolerance.

In February 313 Licinius met Constantine at Milan, and there married Constantine's sister. At this meeting a policy of complete religious freedom was agreed upon; the corporation of the Christian Church—or rather, perhaps, of each separate Christian Church—was recognized as a legal person; the text was doubtless settled of a rescript which would be put into force by Licinius on his return to the East. It is that text which is generally known as the Edict of Milan. Seeck has shown that we cannot prove that there ever was an Edict published at Milan; it is indeed unlikely that any such edict was issued, but this is so because in all probability Constantine had anticipated the agreement in policy reached at Milan in rescripts similar to that directed to Anullinus, which had been sent to all the governors of the Western provinces. The Edict of Milan may be a fiction, but the fact for which the term stood remains untouched. Licinius left Milan to carry to the Christians of the East the message of toleration, recognition, and restitution framed by the senior Augustus. He was met by the revolt of his Caesar Maximin; after Maximin's defeat and death the mastery of the Roman world was shared between Licinius and Constantine.

Only a few months had passed since the victory of the Milvian Bridge when Constantine's exclusion of the Donatists from the imperial benefactions was challenged: the schismatics appealed to the emperor praying that he would appoint judges from Gaul to settle the dispute. Constantine accepted the petition, chose three Gallic bishops, and wrote to the Pope and a certain Marcus directing them, together with their Gallic colleagues, to examine the ten Donatist and ten Catholic representatives from Africa and thus determine the issue. It is, says Constantine, very grievous to him that a large number of his subjects in lands which the divine providence has entrusted to him should be found persistently turning to vanity (ἐπὶ τὸ φαυλότερον) and that bishops should be at variance with one another. The Pope and Marcus are to rest assured that Constantine pays such reverence to the lawfully constituted Catholic Church that he desires that they should nowhere leave in any place schism or discord. The emperor, you will observe, has set up an ecclesiastical tribunal of five judges; the Pope, following the practice of the Church, transforms this tribunal into a council by adding fourteen Italian bishops. This is important, for in the following year Constantine shows by summoning the Council of Arles [August 1, 314] that he has learnt his lesson. . . .

The Council of Arles reaffirmed the judgment of Rome: once more the Donatists protested and petitioned the emperor personally to judge the issue. The letter which the emperor sent to the bishops assembled at Arles before they returned to their sees is of great significance for the biography of Constantine; the whole letter deserves careful study. I can quote only a few extracts:

"The incomprehensible kindness of our God"—note the pronoun—"by no means allows the state of man to stray for too long a time in the darkness, nor does it suffer the odious wills of some so to prevail as not to grant men a new opportunity for conversion to the truth (iustitiam) by opening up before them through its most glorious light a path to salvation. Of this indeed I am assured by many examples and I can illustrate the same truth from my own case. For at the first there were in me things which appeared far removed from the truth (iustitia carere) and I did not think that there was any heavenly power which could see into the secrets of my heart. What fortune ought these things which I have mentioned to have brought upon me?—surely one overflowing with every evil. But Almighty God, Who

sitteth in the watch-tower of Heaven, has bestowed upon me that which I did not deserve.
Truly, most holy bishops of the Saviour Christ,
at this time I can neither describe nor number
these gifts which of His heavenly benevolence
He has granted to me, his servant *(famulum
suum)."*

The emperor congratulates the bishops
on their decision which should recall to
the truth those whom the malignity of the
devil seemed to have alienated from the
glorious light of the Catholic law *(legis
catholicae),* who in their war against the
truth had joined themselves to the gen-
tiles *(gentibus):*

> "But that judgement has been of no avail
> since so great a madness holds the Donatists
> captive that with unbelievable arrogance they
> persuade themselves of things which may not
> be said or heard, departing from the right
> judgement which has been given, from which,
> as by Heaven's provision I have learnt, they
> are appealing to my judgement. Oh! what
> force has the wickedness which still persists
> in their breasts. . . . They ask judgement from
> me who am myself awaiting the judgement of
> Christ; for I declare, as is the truth, that the
> judgement of bishops ought to be looked upon
> as if the Lord Himself were sitting in judge-
> ment. . . . They have instituted an appeal as is
> done in the lawsuits of the pagans; for pagans
> are accustomed at times to avoid the lower
> courts where justice can be quickly discerned
> and through the intervention of the authorities
> to resort to an appeal to the higher courts.
> What is to be said of these defamers of the law
> who rejecting the judgement of Heaven have
> thought that they should demand judgement
> from me? Do they thus think of Christ the
> Saviour? They are self-confessed betray-
> ers. . . . Do you return to your own sees. As
> for these wicked deceivers of religion I have
> given instructions to my men to bring them to
> my court that there they may stay and may
> behold something worse than death. And I
> have sent letters to the vicarius of Africa with
> orders that as often as he finds any sharing in
> this madness he should send them at once to

my court, lest under so great a shining of our
God they should be guilty of spreading further
that which may arouse the greatest wrath of
the Providence of Heaven."

You will notice the recurrence of this
thought. That fear does, I feel, form a
vital element in Constantine's religious
policy. . . .

The story is not usually told at this
length in our textbooks, and yet to my
mind it is the essential prelude to the understanding of Constantine's conduct after
his conquest of the East from Licinius.
The eastern Augustus had felt that his
Christian subjects looked with envious
eyes upon the men of the West governed
by an emperor who made no secret of his
devotion to the Christian God; gradually
Licinius drifted into a petty persecution
of the Christians; the martyrs were few,
and those did not perish by the orders of
Licinius, but through the officious zeal of
his agents. Yet once more the Civil Service was purified of Christians, and Christians were forced to participate in pagan
ceremonies. The war between the two
Augusti, fought in A.D. 323, is represented
as a religious war in the history of Eusebius, and I see no reason to doubt that
such was its character in the eyes of Constantine. The defeat of Licinius was
straightway followed by the issue of two
edicts preserved in a Greek version by
Eusebius in his panegyric on Constantine.
The authenticity of these texts is still
denied by many scholars, though I think
without good reason. We have seen that
immediately after the Battle of the Milvian Bridge Constantine had granted
privileges to the Christians, so now after
the battle of Chrysopolis the emperor
declares that his policy remains un-
changed. In the former of the two edicts
Constantine first deals with the restoration to the Christians of personal rights

and then of rights to property. The edict is the great measure of "liquidation" terminating the whole period of the persecutions from A.D. 303 onward. Constantine knew in what way Maximin had interpreted the edict of toleration issued by Galerius: had Licinius secured a faithful application of the religious policy which had been agreed upon at Milan? In any event doubts should be ended, and a comprehensive measure should inaugurate the new régime. We may presume that Constantine was familiar with the work of Lactantius—he had summoned the Christian rhetorician from the East to Gaul to be the tutor of his son—and the argument of the *De Mortibus Persecutorum* had just been signally vindicated: Licinius proclaiming the policy concerted at Milan had overthrown the persecutor Maximin, Licinius turned persecutor had been dethroned by Constantine. The edict begins with a lengthy exposition of the theme of Lactantius' pamphlet. "Trivialities," says Seeck, but whether you believe this philosopher of human history or not, you must surely confess that the vision of Jewish prophet and Christian apologist of a God living in and through human history is a majestic conception; you will admit that, should a ruler happen to believe it, it must have for him a greater practical significance than any other consideration. For the evils of the age of persecution God had found the remedy in Constantine:

"God sought my service and judged that service fitted to achieve His purpose. Starting from Britain God had scattered the evil powers that mankind might be recalled to true religion instructed through my agency, and that the blessed faith might spread under His guiding hand. And from the West, believing that this gift had been entrusted to myself, I have come to the East which was in sorer need of my aid. At the same time I am absolutely persuaded that I owe my whole life, my every breath, and in a word my most secret thoughts to the supreme God."

Do you not catch the echo? Constantine had once imagined that no divine power could penetrate to the secrets of his heart. It would be strange, Constantine proceeds, if the glory of the confessors should not be raised to greater splendour and blessedness under the rule of the servant of God. . . .

The second of the two edicts preserved by Eusebius is a confession of faith. It begins with a repetition of the argument derived from the melancholy deaths of the persecutors: the violence of the polytheist ending in destruction, the mercy and the piety of Constantine's father the monotheist, the worshipper of the Saviour God, transmitting his rule to his son. Constantine's sense of his mission is reasserted; he prays God to grant to the much tried eastern provinces healing through His servant:

"Not unreasonably do I make this prayer to Thee, Lord of the Universe, Holy God. Under Thy leading have I attempted and accomplished deeds which have brought salvation (σωτηριώδη πράγματα); everywhere with Thy seal as my protection (i.e the sign of the cross on the Christian standard, the labarum) I have led my army to victory, and, if the need of the state should summon me, following the same symbols of Thy virtue, I will go forth against the foe."

But the real interest of the edict lies in Constantine's declaration of policy towards the pagans. His desire is that his people should remain in peace and concord for the common advantage of the inhabited world and of all men. "Let those who are in error be free to enjoy the same peace and quietude as those who believe. Let no one molest another; let each hold to that which his soul desires and let him use this to the full. But as for the wise—it is right that they should be persuaded that those alone will live a holy and pure life whom Thou, O God, callest to find rest in Thy holy laws." Later he repeats the same counsel adding, "For it is one thing to enter voluntarily upon the struggle for immortality, another to compel others to do so from fear of punishment." He has explained his position at length, "since some think, as I hear, that the rites of the temples and the power of darkness have been abolished. That indeed I would have recommended to all men if it had not been that the violent revolt of wicked error were not immoderately fixed in the minds of some to the injury of the common salvation." There is, it should freely be admitted, no precise parallel elsewhere in Constantine's writings to this expression of policy, but the same spirit of scornful tolerance breathes through not a few of his edicts. As the years passed toleration of paganism gave place to active repression; the emperor felt that he was strong enough to advance to a frontal attack upon paganism. The important fact to realize, however, is that this alteration in policy entailed no change of spirit, only a change of method. What Constantine would have recommended in 323 he later felt free to proclaim as the imperial will. The emperor, addressing the world of his new pagan subjects in the eastern provinces, allays their fears by announcing toleration for the old believers; those who deny the authenticity of the edict have no easy task before them when they seek a plausible motive for the falsification of the document.

Constantine had come to the East with high hopes; he found the Eastern Church rent by the Arian controversy. Would there be in the Christian East another Donatist schism? He sent his trusted counsellor Hosius of Cordova to Alexan-

dria with a letter addressed to the bishop Alexander and the presbyter Arius. This is a very remarkable document. In it Constantine first states his aims in marching to the East: one was to heal the body of the Roman world which was suffering from a severe wound; that aim was achieved by military force in the overthrow of Licinius; the other was to unite his subjects in one common religious belief. "I knew that, if in accordance with my prayers I could establish a common agreement amongst all the servants of God, then the need of the state would as the friut of that agreement undergo a change in consonance with the pious desires of all." The only way in which it seemed to the emperor possible to cure the Donatist disorders was that envoys from the Eastern Church should be sent to Africa on a mission of conciliation. Christianity had arisen in the East and thence spread through the world; the Easterners were therefore the natural missionaries for the world's salvation. "No sooner was the victory achieved than my first inquiry was directed to this end which I thought to be of greater value and moment than anything else." The bitter disappointment of the failure in Africa had left its mark upon the soul of Constantine.

And now, in place of union, battles of words about abstruse points which might perhaps have provided an exercise for philosophic debate, but should rather be kept imprisoned in the mind, not rashly made public nor thoughtlessly disclosed to the ears of the multitude. Let Alexander and Arius take a lesson from the philosophers who if they disagree on *one* point still act in concert to maintain the unity of philosophic doctrine. How much more should we who are constituted servants of the great God be of one mind in the fundamental beliefs of our religion! Constantine offers himself as a mediator of peace in this dispute: he pleads that he, the servant of God—a phrase now familiar to us—may be allowed under Providence to bring God's people by his words and help and counsel to a renewed communion. The emperor had hoped to visit the provinces won from Licinius, but was restrained from so doing that he might not be compelled to see with his own eyes things which even to hear of he had thought an impossibility. "Open to me by your unity the road to the East!" For our purpose the letter is of interest as evidence of Constantine's conviction that he was called to play the part of providential mediator between the disputants.

The mission of Hosius failed; bishops assembled at Antioch condemned Arius and fixed on Ancyra as the town in which a larger council should assemble to formulate with greater authority the standpoint of the Eastern Church. Ancyra was the see of Marcellus, the champion of the extreme view diametrically opposed to that of Arius. The emperor, who had expressed the desire to act as mediator, should be faced with a *fait accompli*. It was shrewd tactics, but Constantine, who naturally did not desire the victory of either extreme, was equal to the occasion. He commandeered the Council of Ancyra by proposing to make it not merely representative of the Eastern Church, but oecumenical in its range. Then, having possessed himself of the initiative, he transferred the council to Nicaea where its deliberations would be subject to his own control. At that council, I believe, Constantine acted as President and as such directed its proceedings towards the adoption of his own solution—the Homoousion.[1] Whence Constantine derived that solution we need not ask here: it may well

have come not from Hosius, but from some eastern adviser of the emperor. . . . The solution was so successful that the council found it necessary to excommunicate only two bishops.

The letters written after Nicaea[2] are filled with Constantine's gratitude for the success of his efforts to secure unity. "From the divine Providence we have received fulness of grace that we may, freed from all error, acknowledge one and the same faith. No longer can the devil work his will against us," his plots have been overthrown by the bishops, and in that triumph Constantine could claim no small share. "That this end might be attained, by the will of God I summoned to the city of Nicaea as many bishops as possible with whom I, your fellow-servant, as one of your number rejoiced above measure to be present and myself received the exposition of the truth." To those bishops who were not at the council he wrote: "Having learned from the prosperity of the state how great is the favour of the divine power, I considered that before everything else my aim should be that among the most blessed congregations of the Catholic Church there should be observed one faith, love unalloyed, and piety towards God, the Lord of all, unsullied by discord." . . .

Such is the evidence to be derived from the letters and edicts of Constantine; its cumulative effect would appear to me to be of considerable weight. I will not weaken that effect by any lengthy comment. But to my mind one or two conclusions do naturally present themselves and these may be briefly formulated. The letters and edicts of Constantine are not the writings of one who was merely a philosophical monotheist whose faith was de-

---

[1] The view that the Father (God) and the Son (Christ) were "of one essence."—Ed.

[2] The Council of Nicaea convened on May 20, 325.—Ed.

rived from the religious syncretism of his day—a faith into which Christianity had been absorbed. Salvatorelli's view cannot, I believe, be maintained. The emperor has definitely identified himself with Christianity, with the Christian Church and the Christian creed. Further, here is a sovereign with the conviction of a personal mission entrusted to him by the Christian God—a mission which imposes duties; it is a charge which he cannot escape, if he would. In the third place, in Constantine's thought the prosperity of the Roman state is intimately, one may, I think, say necessarily, linked to the cause of unity within the Catholic Church. If God is to do His part, the Emperor and the Christian Church must render to him in return—as ἀμοιβή [compensation]— the loyalty of concord. Here, I believe, is to be found the determining factor in the religious policy of the emperor—his aim was ever to establish unity in the Catholic Church. After his failure in Africa he found the basis of union in the Homoou- sion of the Council of Nicaea, and that formulation of Christian doctrine he persistently and consistently maintained. He has been accused of weakness and of hesitation in the execution of his religious policy; yet in his purpose he never wa- vered, though he might vary the means chosen for its realization; he knew that it was idle in the cause of unity to create schism. We think of Constantine as the enemy of Athanasius. That is perhaps because we read the history of the time through the eyes of Athanasius. Con- stantine supported the Eusebian party because that party stood for inclusion, while Athanasius was the representative of a policy of exclusion. The Eusebians were willing to restore schismatics— the Melitians—and heretics—the Ari- ans—when they had repented of their errors, and Athanasius was not so willing. Constantine's vision was that of a Roman Empire sustained by a Christian God and founded on an orthodox faith. That vision was ultimately realized in the New Rome which he had founded. Constantine, the *religiosissimus Augustus,* has his place amongst the seers and the prophets. It was not altogether unfitting that he should be laid to rest in the Church of the Twelve Apostles, himself the thirteenth Apostle.

Constantine's religious development is the subject of the following selection by J.-R. PALANQUE (b. 1898), professor of ancient history at Aix-en-Provence. Palanque argues that Constantine's religious position was the product of an evolutionary, rather than a cataclysmic, decision. Rejecting the political and syncretic interpretations of Constantine's "conversion," he suggests that the emperor was "one of those minds . . . in which a sincere mysticism is combined with a boundless ambition."*

J.-R. Palanque

# Progressive Conversion

## Historical Testimonies to the Conversion of Constantine

The two emperors who in 313 divided the Roman Empire between them . . . agreed in protecting Christianity. What were the motives of so sudden a change of policy? Ecclesiastical tradition very soon explained it by the miracle of a sudden and complete conversion of Constantine to the Christian religion. Quite apart from the later legend, according to which the conqueror of Maxentius was welcomed in Rome by Pope Silvester, received baptism from him, and then conferred upon the Pope a veritable sovereignty over the Eternal City—a legend as unacceptable as the pagan version given by Zosimus, who likewise places in Rome the adoption of Christianity by the Emperor, but under date 326—there are some well-known texts which narrate certain marvellous events which are said to have led Constantine to embrace the Christian Faith. According to Lactantius and Eusebius, a message from the Almighty revealed the Christian Religion to the prince during the campaign of 312, and Constantine thereupon gave plain signs of his conversion.

Lactantius mentions briefly a dream on the eve of the decisive battle of the 27th of October: "Constantine was warned during his sleep to carve upon his shields the heavenly sign from God, and then to

*From J.-R. Palanque et al. *The Church in the Christian Roman Empire* (London: Burns & Oates, Ltd., 1949), pp. 12–24, translated by E. C. Messenger. Footnotes omitted.

engage in the combat. He did as he was commanded and . . . he carved the Christ upon his shields."

Eusebius, in his sermon at the dedication of the church at Tyre, about 316, speaks of the two emperors as zealous Christians who "spat in the faces of the dead idols . . . and derided the old error which had been handed down," and who "confessed the Christ . . . proclaiming Him to be the Saviour on the standards." In his *Ecclesiastical History,* written about 325, he gives an equally enthusiastic and vague eulogy, but of Constantine alone, who, "adhering quite naturally to the religion of God," engaged in combat with Maxentius only after praying to the God of Heaven and Jesus Christ, and who, after his victory, bore witness to his faith by erecting in the most populous place in Rome his own statue with a cross in his hand.

Finally, in his *Life of Constantine,* the same Eusebius describes at length, according to information given him by the prince himself, a miraculous episode which apparently took place at the beginning of the campaign of 312. One afternoon, Constantine had a vision, in presence of the whole army, of a shining cross in the sky, together with the words: "In this sign thou shalt conquer." On the next night, he received in a dream the order to copy this sign; on the morrow these apparitions were explained by Christian priests, and a standard was made in accordance with the divine command. In Philostorgius we have a narrative of a similar vision, seen in the night-time.

### Difficulties in the Narratives

These various testimonies, which are somewhat discordant, give rise to a number of problems. The statements in Eusebius's *History* are full of inexactitudes: Licinius was never a Christian, and Con-

stantine himself had in no wise repudiated paganism, especially at the date in question. Yet this text would lead one to suppose that he had always been quite naturally a Christian. As to the Roman statue with the cross, it is to be feared that the historian of Caesarea mistook the signification of this monument, and that its Christian character rests entirely on a misunderstanding of the imperial *vexillum,* and an ambiguity in the inscription on the pedestal. And as to the account in the *De vita Constantini,* there is strong ground for suspecting that it contains fantastic embellishments. Might not the vision of the Cross in full daylight be a natural meteoric phenomenon? A possibly true incident may have been given a number of most unlikely developments by the imagination of the historian, or of the emperor himself. The standard, which is minutely described, is simply the Constantinian *labarum,* found also on coins; it is certain that it could not have been made in the course of the lightning campaign of 312, for the time and artists were lacking at that date. Further, is it possible that Constantine was unable to understand the significance of the cross without the explanations of the priests? "It is difficult to admit that he was so ignorant of Christianity until that time?" Lastly, the details given scarcely harmonise with the testimony of Lactantius.

### Denials of the Conversion:
### Constantine as a Mere Politician

These textual difficulties certainly render the problem of Constantine's conversion a singularly difficult one. Some historians have solved it in a categorical manner by denying the reality or sincerity of the conversion. Among these, a first group is constituted by those who think that Constantine, personally without religion, utilised religion in the interests of his policy. From Gibbon in the 18th century down to our time, this system has found powerful defenders, who complain that the strong personality of the prince has been misrepresented by the least intelligent and the least honest of the writers of panegyrics, or else they explain the whole Constantinian history by the "will to power" in their hero. This radical idea is open to very serious objections. If Constantine studied only his own interests, apart from any personal conviction, what advantage could it have been to him to displease the great majority of his subjects by joining a religion despised both by the masses and by the *élite?* Again, it is pointed out that a great and ambitious man is not necessarily a sceptic, and moreover, a freethinker would indeed be a *rara avis* in the fourth century. This makes it doubly unlikely that Constantine was a mere politician.

Yet that is the thesis which H. Grégoire has recently supported by new arguments. To those who are impressed by the testimonies of contemporary Christian writers, he replies that the account of Lactantius must be a transposition of a pagan vision alluded to in a Panegyric of 310, and that the account in the *De vita Constantini* is merely an interpolation belonging to the second half of the fourth century and without any historical value. As for Constantine's interests in this matter, he thinks he can account for these by formulating an ingenious historical law, which applies to all the emperors of that time: "What determined their actions was not so much a desire to respect the faith of their immediate subjects as a wish to draw to themselves the mass of the soldiers and civilians in the parts of the Empire over which they hoped to extend their sway." In particular, Constantine, he suggests, made advances to the Christians in 312 in order to conciliate those

living in the states of Maxentius, just as in 324 he took a similar step in regard to the subjects of Licinius.

However ingenious and powerful this explanation may be, we regard it as nothing more than a brilliant paradox, founded on questionable postulates. Certainly the history of the Church would not be radically disturbed if one were to accept it, and it may well be that "this somewhat revolutionary conception of the history of the triumph of Christianity" would in no wise lessen "its pathetic majesty." Even so, it seems difficult to accept this refinement of criticism concerning Lactantius and Eusebius and this much too systematic "historical law," which simply manifests the bias already pointed out: it is hardly likely that mere political opportunism suffices to explain the religious attitude of all the emperors!

## Constantine as a "Syncretist"

Accordingly another group of historians, without refusing to believe in Constantine's sincerity, regard him as a religious man, but one who was only half a Christian. Accepting, as his father did, the Syncretistic Theism of his time, he sought, according to this view, to graft Christianity on to the vague paganism he professed, and his ignorance and superstition, no less than a desire to please all the world, led him to adopt an equivocal attitude, which lasted until 324, if not until his death. This thesis has a certain historical probability; it is based in particular on undeniable facts, such as the pagan character of the official texts (formulae of the Panegyrics, coins and inscriptions) and the retaining of the pagan pontificate among the imperial offices. But it makes the mistake of entirely neglecting the Christian testimonies. This is done, for instance, by A. Piganiol, who, adopting the critical attitude of H. Grégoire, rejects the account in Lactantius as a mere "Christian adaptation" of the "authentic" pagan vision in 310, and represents Constantine as a superstitious man hesitating between the divergent interpretations of the magical signs he had adopted, and a follower at once of solar myths, Gnosticism, and the Christian Faith—in brief, down to his death "a muddled man who was groping his way." But in our opinion, this is to extend too far the undoubted hesitations in Constantine's mind, and above all, it misrepresents the mental outlook of the great emperor who was a sincere Syncretist at first, a cautious politician throughout his life, but also a convinced Christian after 312.

## Character of Constantine

His Christianity certainly needs to be defined, and his conversion calls for explanation and for distinctions. Between the uncritical panegyrists and the historians who, though not rejecting his conversion, paint a picture of him full of scorn and contempt, there is room for an analysis which will endeavour to remain within the bounds of likelihood and at the same time will respect the requirements of criticism.

The character of Constantine was above all that of a strong and bold man: to the Army he was a trainer of men, and a bold strategist; in the Court he liked display and magnificence; he acted as a man of culture with a lofty mind, and always took delight in action and creation. He desired to astonish men and to win the hearts of his subjects, and also to retain the attention of posterity. In order to satisfy his ambition, or merely his vanity, he spared neither reforms nor expenses, without thinking of the consequences or reactions, for usually his decisions were made on the spur of the moment. He was impulsive, open to influence, but also profoundly conscious of his mission. His will to dominate was upheld and increased by the consciousness of his duty and his confidence in his destiny: he trusted in his star, for he felt that he was directed by divine forces. He was a great politician, and in no wise a cold calculator confined within systems or intrigues; he was one of those minds, powerful though confused and superstitious, in which a sincere mysticism is combined with a boundless ambition. He did not separate his own interests from the service of the State or from that of his God, for he regarded himself as the visible representative of both. Hence we can understand that, in his religious evolution, political motives, which were more or less present to his mind, were combined with convictions which were certainly sincere. The object of his worship changed indeed, but not his temperament.

## The Stages in His Conversion

It was by successive stages that he reached Christianity, and not through the illumination of a single day. We find in him precisely the three degrees of conversion mentioned by Lactantius in one of his works: "The first (degree) judges the false religions and rejects impious cults; the second discovers that there is only one supreme God; the third reveals the minister whom this God sent on earth in order to announce Him."

## Solar Syncretism

The first stage was merely a purified form of paganism which, it would seem, Constantine inherited from his father Constantius. For the latter, who, in the words of an ecclesiastical historian, "turned away from the Hellenic cults," professed the Solar Syncretism made fashionable by the philosophers and pagan mystics of the third century, and in particular, he worshipped under the name of Apollo the heavenly divinity who was as popular in his own native Illyria as in the Gaul he ruled. We may reasonably ascribe the same beliefs to Constantius's son. When he acceded to the imperial office in 306, reasons of State compelled him to honour the gods of the Tetrarchy, Jupiter and Hercules, and particularly the former, the patron of Maximian, whose daughter he married. But in 310 when, having broken with his father-in-law, he substituted for the "Heraclean" dynasty a new lawful succession, and this official dynasty of the "second Flavians," supposed to have sprung from Claudius the Goth, had as its official dynasty the *Sol invictus*. In this connection, some have spoken of a "first conversion" of Constantine; it would perhaps be more correct to see here a return to his family and personal beliefs, no longer affected by respect for the Tetrarchy.

## Philosophical Monotheism

The second stage, that of Monotheism, was, moreover, reached already in 311: the official phraseology of the *Panegyrics,* setting aside all mythology, renders homage now only to "the Divine Spirit by which the universe is governed," and which has its symbolical incarnation, as it were, in the sun. If we may rely on many literary and numismatic texts, the prince must have remained a long time in this philosophical belief, expressed in Stoic or Neoplatonist terms but animated by a real religious spirit. This "sovereign Creator" is invoked in the *Panegyric* of 313 and the prince appeals to the *divinitas,* himself being *invictus,* like the god of his empire.

## A Superstitious Christianity

Yet Constantine in 312 passed on to the third stage: apart from Eusebius, whose account one must definitely set aside, Lactantius, whose veracity can scarcely be doubted, bears express witness to this fact: in consequence of a dream, the emperor caused a Christian emblem to be carved on the shields of his soldiers. Engaged as he was in a very dangerous enterprise, on the eve of a decisive battle, and lacking the support of the pagan powers, who seemed to withdraw themselves, this was without doubt merely the superstitious action of a gambler, who wished to test a mysterious force. Had not the Christian God already proved His "virtue" by causing the most fearful persecution to collapse? Was it not desirable to consider Him and to propitiate Him? Victory followed upon this appeal, motivated by interest. Constantine saw definitely in Christ the envoy of the supreme God, whom he had already worshipped under the form of the sun. This belief was as yet "only a beginning of Christianity"; for his new devotion was not at first separated from his former belief: his "conversion," far from being a break with the past, was but the culmination and confirmation of his own ideas. Why then should he abandon the language he had hitherto used, especially as its vagueness would give satisfaction to enlightened pagans? We can understand that the official phraseology remained vaguely monotheistic, and that the *Sol invictus* continued to be honoured, especially as this could be regarded as a quasi-Christian symbol, and at the very least as harmless. In an Empire still containing a majority of pagans, and with a colleague himself pagan, such equivocal conduct would be the most diplomatic attitude to adopt, if not the only possible one.

The unconscious Syncretism of a convert not fully aware of the exigencies of his faith, and the conscious desire to please the polytheistic majority and his cultivated subjects suffice to explain the "pagan survivals" which one finds in Constantine after 312. Similarly, the desire to safeguard the independence of the State and the imperial sovereignty prevented him from being baptised and from giving up the pagan pontificate. He thus retained a footing in both camps, and down to the day of his death he remained, strictly speaking, outside the Church, and not even a catechumen, much less a member. But all this must not lead us to reject the reality of his conversion: from 312 Constantine believed in the redeeming Christ, and he adopted His monogram for the shields of his soldiers, even before he fixed it on his helmet and his standard, and depicted it on his coins. Again, from 312 he was devoted to the Church, which he honoured, protected and favoured in every way possible. In this way we can explain the new religious policy which he began to apply in January 313, and which was the subject of an agreement with Licinius on the occasion of their meeting at Milan in the following month.

In the following selection ANDREAS ALFÖLDI (b. 1895), professor of Roman history in the Institute for Advanced Study, Princeton, New Jersey, and one of the most provocative scholars of the later Roman Empire, argues that Constantine was a credulous man who sincerely believed that the Christian God had provided special assistance in his crucial battle with Maxentius. Especially worth noting here are Alfoldi's attitude toward the ancient literary accounts of the conversion, his use of numismatic evidence, and the emphasis on later "Christian" actions of the emperor, which, in Alfoldi's judgment, attest his conversion.*

**Andreas Alföldi**

## *Wrapped in the Darkness of Superstition*

Ever since modern rationalism opened its campaign of "enlightenment" against the Church, while the Church has reacted to its attacks with a vigorous defence, both parties have been trying, consciously or unconsciously, to fit the conversion of the first Christian Emperor into their own scheme and to interpret it accordingly. And what has been the result? The moderns have declined to reach their understanding of Constantine's fateful resolve from the conditions of late antiquity, from the spiritual state of the fourth century, from its proper environment, in fact. Generation after generation has shifted its valuation of that decisive step of Constantine, nay, more, of his whole life-work, to suit its own point of view, has involuntarily but relentlessly modernized it. Even to-day this procedure has not yet reached its end.

The farthest departure from historical fact has, in my opinion, been achieved by those who have tried to obliterate the miracle of the *hoc signo victor eris* with the drastic thoroughness of the housewife, who used such a powerful acid to take the stain out of her son's coat that she destroyed the cloth as well. The champions of this view have not stopped with the miracle that took place in front of the Mulvian Bridge. With it they have discarded all the plain evidences of the religious fervour that brimmed the heart of Constantine, and have made of him a cynical figure, a divided and hypocritical

*From A. Alföldi, *The Conversion of Constantine and Pagan Rome,* translated by H. Mattingly (Oxford: The Clarendon Press, 1948), pp. 1–4, 16–24. Reprinted by permission of The Clarendon Press, Oxford. Footnotes omitted.

personality who, only late and after long vacillation, placed himself on the Christian side. To justify this procedure all the elaborate resources of modern research have recently been applied. The impeccable documents, preserved in the contemporary Church historian, Eusebius, who from this point of view is entirely reliable, have been branded as forgeries. So, too, have the uniquely valuable deeds that relate to the sectarian movement of the Donatists in Africa. The Christian signs on the official coinage under Constantine have been disposed of by interpretation as ambiguous, if not actual pagan, symbols; or, alternatively, their evidence has been decried on the plea that they derive merely from the irresponsible initiative of subordinate officials. This method will not stand a serious test. It is not even, as we shall see, necessary for those who feel that the irrational element must be completely eliminated from the event in question. Authentic documents, and at least equally authentic, purely official, issues of coins supply us with absolute proof that the Emperor embraced the Christian cause with a suddenness that surprised all but his closest intimates. And, even though we may find that the famous vision was not enacted before the eyes of the whole world but only in the Emperor's dream, it was an experience real to him, which had historical effects of world-wide importance. To try to minimize or cancel its significance is labour lost.

There are many causes in men's own minds that have hindered a right appraisal of Constantine, or have, at the least, given rise to perverse and unjustifiable conceptions of him. But there is also an external cause that has confused judgement on the matter. If you look back on the figure of the Emperor from the Middle Ages and observe how his activities prescribed the fortunes of the Byzantine world for centuries ahead, you get the impression that these vast effects were due to the achievement of a single man, with no historical introduction, no organic development behind him. Seen thus, Constantine is like a mighty rock, jutting skyward out of the sea of history. But if, on the other hand, you begin with the Early Empire and view the course of evolution in the most diverse departments of life from that angle, if you see that evolution, however varied the forms it takes, always describing the same upward and downward curve, you are left without any doubt that every step taken by Constantine simply supplied a reasonable solution to problems already existing and just grown ripe for settlement; and that those steps must have been taken by the occupants of the throne—perhaps decades later, perhaps in somewhat different form—but taken without fail.

For those rulers of nations who have exercised a decisive influence on the shaping of human destinies have certainly not been all men of a single kind. One you find raised to the dizzy height of a throne by his own authentic greatness. Another gains recognition by the sheer weight of his rude, barbarian energies. Many have simply been lifted on the tides of mass emotion or brought to the helm of State at the critical moment by other circumstances, outside their control. Such men have had no more difficulty in discharging their role in history than those high-born ladies who have only to press a trembling finger on a button for the iron colossus of a battleship to glide smoothly into the sea.

Constantine, indeed, was not privileged to pluck his laurels so easily. There had already been one Emperor before him who had determined for centuries in advance the path that the Roman Empire was to tread, the Emperor Augustus. Just as Constantine had had his mighty forerunner in the person of Diocletian, so too, as we all know, Julius Caesar had smoothed the way for the constitutional reforms of Augustus. Augustus, like Constantine, if we look back on his reign from the vantage-point of after-ages, appears to us as the man who held the initiative at every point in the reform of State and society. And yet, in his case, too, it becomes clear, as we test what lay behind his activities, that his lofty conception of the Principate had already been sketched out for him by Cicero; clear, too, that he was only able to give a lasting shape to the Roman Empire because a mighty historical development had just reached maturity. But despite these striking parallels, Constantine is left far behind by Augustus. Look at the brilliant imitative art of the talented Claudius Claudianus—how it pales before the unique, unspoiled Roman gift of Virgil! Look, again, at the organic modelling, the delicate individualization of the portraits of the Augustan age—how they throw into the shade, from the point of view of creative art, the grandiose but mechanical head of Constantine on his Basilica in Rome! What a distance separates the artistic refinements of an Arretine pot of the Augustan age from the rough, though decorative, figures of an African pot of the fourth century! Just the same distance is to be seen between the value of the achievements of the two Emperors. What Constantine achieved might, under favourable circumstances, have been accomplished—and with more tact—by the highly gifted, much traduced, Gallienus. Even the coarse but worthy and consistent Aurelian was equal to such tasks. But the work of Augustus was the unique creation of a superior spirit, and it could never be repeated.

It cannot be our aim to record the many

mutually exclusive conceptions that have been formed of the Emperor who first inscribed the name of Christ on his banner. Enough if we realize that research in the last three centuries has, for all its contradictions and controversies, achieved immense progress. The old familiar sources have been thoroughly scoured, new sources have been discovered and made available for study; scholars of the most diverse schools have contributed valuable observations and results that will stand. Wide perspectives have been opening out before us. We have already to hand a considerable number of pieces of many-coloured mosaic. If, after a careful sorting, we can add a few new stones and put them all back, without prejudice, in their right, original places, the genuine character of the victory of Christ is bound to appear. . . .

Most of us are familiar with the account given by Eusebius, Bishop of Caesarea, of the conversion of Constantine a quarter of a century after the event. According to his account the Almighty gave ear to Constantine's fervent prayer and sent him a divine sign of wonder in the sky. Above the setting sun the Emperor, and his army with him, saw the sign of the Cross, outlined in rays of light, and, with it, the words: "In this sign thou shalt conquer." He did not at first understand the vision—so he maintained on oath to Eusebius—until Christ appeared to him in a dream and commanded him to copy the sign that he had seen in the sky and use it in battle as a talisman of defence. Constantine obeyed and ordered that a standard made of gold and studded with sparkling jewels should be prepared, to bring salvation and protect from harm. Henceforward it was borne at the head of all his armies. He likewise caused the initial letters of the Redeemer's name to be set on his helmet and continued to bear them there. Deeply impressed by the wonder that he had seen, Constantine summoned Christian priests to him. They taught him about Christ and explained that the Cross was the symbol of victory over death. Convinced by their interpretation of the miracle that a divine revelation had indeed been vouchsafed to him, Constantine became anxious to occupy himself with the reading of Holy Writ and, by every means in his power, to serve the God whom he had beheld. It was full of good hope, then, that he went into battle against the blood-stained and dissolute tyrant. In reliance on the help of God he gained victory after victory. And, as once the Lord, to protect Moses and his God-fearing people, had cast Pharaoh and his war-chariots and the might of his army into the sea, and had sunk his chosen leaders in the Red Sea, so now Maxentius with his bodyguard sank "in the deeps like a stone" when, fleeing before the might of the God who fought for Constantine, he tried to escape over the bridge of boats. The jubilant song of the soldiers rose sky-high.

Towards the close of his life, when his whole being was flooded with religious enthusiasm, Constantine represented all these events as a succession of miracles, following on the revelation vouchsafed him—just as though there had been no bloody slaughters for him to execute, but he had simply made a pilgrimage in which faith worked the wonders. The pompous and exaggerated style of Eusebius gives it away. The historian doubtless contributed the fine flowers of his own piety to adorn the story as heard from the Emperor. But, objectively regarded, the course of events was much more commonplace, more true to normal human experience, than that edifying story in all its dazzling colours. But it was no whit less important in its consequences.

Not that Eusebius' account has no kernel of historical fact. We can prove beyond a doubt, by the evidence of coin-types appearing soon after, that Constantine caused the monogram of Christ to be inscribed on his helmet before the decisive battle with Maxentius. Again, it is an assured fact that the banner with the sign of Christ became the sacred ensign of the armies of Constantine and, afterwards, of the Christian Empire in general. But a comparison of the description of Eusebius with the rest of the evidence shows that it is marred by one particular misunderstanding, which is quite easy to explain. It was not the Cross that appeared in the vision, but the monogram of Christ, consisting of the letters Chi Rho. A much better attested version of the vision which partly completes, partly corrects, that of Eusebius is found in Lactantius, the Christian rhetorician who, not long after these events, became the tutor of the eldest son of Constantine and wrote his pamphlet on the "Deaths of the Persecutors." In his account the wonder did not take place anywhere in Gaul or in broad daylight, but immediately before the battle of the Mulvian Bridge. The Emperor, in a dream, saw the initial letters of the name of Christ and the words of light, *Hoc signo victor eris.* Further, we are told, Christ instructed Constantine not only to bear the sign of wonder on his helmet, but also to have it painted on the shields of his soldiers. According to Lactantius, the sign was represented by a vertical stroke, rounded at the top, drawn through the middle of the Chi. We must interpret this to mean that the Rho, hastily painted on the shields, took the form of a round-headed pin. How exact this observation is is proved by the precisely similar variation of the monogram on a coin-type, issued about A.D. 320 in many mints, on instructions from headquarters.

The divine announcement—"In this sign thou shalt conquer"—is an historical fact, then, seen though it was only in a dream. That it was an overwhelming experience, not an ingenious invention to cheat the masses, is proved beyond a doubt by the over-mastering enthusiasm with which Constantine ever afterwards fought for the cause of Christ and His Church.

It was not merely nervous excitability before the decisive battle that made Constantine receptive to visions. We know that he experienced divine instruction in dreams on other occasions when he had important decisions to make. He himself referred the foundation of his new capital to a suggestion of this kind from heaven. Nor was he alone in his age in believing that the heavenly powers are wont to use this means of directing men how they shall act. Countless votive offerings still record how their givers did this or that on divine instruction, received in a dream. Even in the works of Porphyrius, the greatest philosopher of the age, we often encounter kindly spirits and evil demons who guide the life of mortals by visions. This particular Neoplatonist even imagined that the spirits could be invoked and exorcized by art. The leading classes of Christians of the day—Lactantius himself is an example—shared in this conviction; only they expected the supernatural results, not from the conjuration of gods and demons, but from the utterance or showing of the name of Christ and the use of the symbol of the Cross. As the conviction that the gods give such warnings in sleep was so widespread, the fulfilment of the vision that came to Constantine in sleep must have made a deep impression on every hand. The Emperor Licinius, brother-in-law of Constantine, himself tried to trade on this psychological motif, and gave out that he too had had a vision, promising him the victory, when he was about to settle accounts with Maximin Daza. Lactantius, when he wrote, believed that Licinius had had his own enlightenment from on high. But, before long, it proved that the Christian colouring of the religion of Licinius was mere accident and hypocrisy.

It is clear from what we have been saying that the ideas and inferences associated with the vision of Constantine were nothing but abortions of the excitable religious fancy of the late Roman Empire. Constantine was prevented from breaking away from this debased form of religion by his inferior education. Some scholars, indeed, suppose him to have grown up in the atmosphere of the palace and to have realized, from the first, the importance of thorough and individual education of the personality. But such was not the case. The rough, good-tempered Illyrian soldier in whose house Constantine grew up had laid little stress on letting his son have a good education; what he wanted above all was to make him a good general and efficient administrator. At the most, we may allow that Constantine acquired in the air of a palace decent principles of respect for culture, and that this spurred him on to let his own sons have a really thorough classical education.

For all his high birth Constantine was certainly not well educated; he was *litteris minus instructus* [not versed in letters], to quote the words of a reliable authority. A letter of his, it is true, survives, written in beautifully smooth and resonant phrases, which show off the perfect literary education of its composer; but that only makes it the plainer that the brilliant stylist was not the Emperor, who signed it, but a man of letters in the imperial chancellory. What Constantine actually composed himself—letters discussing Christian doctrine and the like—are ponderous and wordy, long-winded compilations. A similar clumsiness and unbridled passion is revealed in his legislation.

If Constantine's acquaintance with worldly literature was slight, his knowledge of the Bible was equally weak. The subtle speculations of theology were a closed book to him. A distinguished modern Church historian has branded his letter to Bishops Alexander and Arius as a forgery, because he was scared by the pieces of "childish silliness" that occur in it. But such primitive ideas characterize the whole of Constantine's religious writings and betray thereby their imperial composition. Proud as Constantine may have been of his wisdom, derived from Smaller Catechisms, loud as may have been the praises of his courtiers for his zealous declaration of faith, thorough as may have been the process of "combing out" to which his written utterances were submitted, it is just these written declarations of Constantine that betray that the dogmatic foundations of Christianity remained a mystery to him.

What really gripped this son of an age of decadence, sunk in superstition and mysticism, was not the refined theological system of the Church, not the lofty moral teaching of the New Testament, but its unbounded faith in the limitless power of Christ. From it he expected the prosperity of his Empire in peace and its victory in war. So true is it that power was for him the deciding factor, that he did not attach himself to Christ until Christ had fulfilled His promise to lend him His aid. . . . From the Christian standpoint, no doubt, this meant a serious decline in the standard of belief. Just before the time of Constantine whole generations of confessors had gladly submitted to the bitterest afflictions from the mighty ones of this world of shadows, to win their rich reward in the hereafter. In complete contrast to

them, the basis of the religious convictions of Constantine was success on earth. His successes in war and peace were represented by him to the world as the proof of the rightness of his confession. Nor was he alone in this. The learned Church historian Eusebius, the highly educated rhetorician and apologist Lactantius, and others with them, said precisely the same, and not a voice was raised in denial.

It is the increasing spread of ideas of primitive religion and magic in that age that explains the exceptional part played in the story of Constantine's conversion by the initial letters of the name of Christ. We see no more in such symbols than purely abstract reminders; but, then, the most palpable magical potency was ascribed to them. Let us listen, for example, to what Lactantius has to say of the amazing efficacy of the sign of the Cross.

How terrified the demons are by this sign may be realized, if you observe how, when conjured by the name of Christ, they take their flight from the bodies that they have possessed. . . . The case is not hard to prove. . . . When the pagans sacrifice to their gods, the sacred act misses its effect, if a single person is present, whose brow is signed with the Cross. This was often the very reason why wicked rulers persecuted the Christian righteousness. When those tyrants were sacrificing and certain of our community were present in their train, those Christian brethren, by signing their brows with the Cross, put the gods to flight, so that they could not reveal the future from the entrails of the beasts. The "haruspices," observing this, at the instigation of those very demons, for whom they were performing their dissections, raised the complaint that "profane" persons were present, disturbing the sacred acts. Thus they moved their princes to fury and drove them to try and storm the Church of God.

The motives that led Diocletian and Galerius to set on foot the persecution of the Church were of a different order, but there can be no doubt that they, too, were troubled by the fear of magic signs. Their eyes, like those of Constantine, were dazzled by the conceptions of a world of mechanical magic, that to us seem so simple-minded. Everyone was then convinced that you could bring the supernatural powers into your service by magic signs, formulas, and rites. Feverish, then, was the quest for such miraculous forms and devices. The Church itself could not quite escape from this atmosphere of fog. We must not fail to notice that Eusebius, for example, regularly describes the divine sign, which, in his account, helped Constantine to victory, as a magic charm. Not only does he place on record all the wonderful tales that Constantine had told him of the miracles performed by the *labarum,* the banner with the initial letters of Christ, but he elaborates them with obvious delight. At a later date Constantine made use of other talismans of Christian character—such as nails from the Redeemer's Cross. One such nail he set in his golden diadem, with its jewelled mount, another in the snaffle of his warhorse. Bishop Ambrose, one of the most brilliant intellects of the century, speaks of such talismans with veneration and wonder. . . . It was no mere accident, either, that our Emperor made trial of the magic power of the Christian monogram just before a battle on the issue of which hung life and death. Human weakness generally turns to heaven when little help can be expected on earth. And there was also a special reason. We have already seen that, since the age of the Antonines, more trust had been placed in the prayers of the Emperor, facing such a decision, than on his arms. The spirit of the age insisted that an Emperor, in such a case, must assure himself of the help of the heavenly powers. From now on it was the victory of the ruler that decided the right-

ness of his religion: that victory was taken as the arbitrament of the true God.

The Christianity of Constantine, then, was not wrapped in the glory of the true Christian spirit, but in the darkness of superstition. But to deny the sincerity and urgency of his religious convictions is to make a very grave mistake. The vision of Constantine swept him off his feet, and its effects far outweighed the bombastic story of wonder in Eusebius.

On the evening of the 27th of October A.D. 312 the monogram, without a spectacular *mise en scène* and with hardly a sound, entered on its brilliant march of triumph. A considerable part of the army hardly knew, it seems, what the sign, painted on their shields, meant. Before the decisive battle was fought, Constantine could not have trumpeted it abroad that he had placed himself and his soldiers under the protection of Christ. He would have been risking a serious reaction on the part of the pagans. At the entry into Rome the sign, conspicuous on the shields of the men, may have begun to arouse attention, may even, here and there, have provoked resentment, but certainly no serious reaction. Nor can Constantine's first measures in favour of the Christians have occasioned any particular excitement in Rome. There had already been the Edict of Toleration and the similar conduct of Maxentius. Constantine's touch was gentle and he was able to avoid any violent convulsions. There was no radio in those days, no loudspeakers or similar instruments of modern publicity, to broadcast exciting news in the twinkling of an eye. The Donatist bishops, as Fr. Stähelin has rightly emphasized, when they wished to flatter Constantine simply declared that they had confidence in him because of his father, who had held back from the persecutions. Of his own Christian confession of faith they said nothing—probably because they knew nothing. More remarkable still is the circumstance that Lactantius, who certainly knew of the new turn of events when he wrote a little later about the "Deaths of the Persecutors," does not celebrate Constantine as the one and only champion of the cause of the Church and as the exclusive favourite of the Lord. Licinius shares in the miraculous aid of God. No one, then, had any idea of how far Constantine intended to go in his favours to the Church. But he himself was quite sure.

The extent to which Constantine's coinage reveals the emperor's commitment to the Christian God is assessed in the following survey by PATRICK BRUUN (b. 1920), director of the Institutum Romanum Findlandiae in Rome and author of several important monographs on fourth-century coinage. Bruun's meticulous analysis certainly is the most comprehensive to date and doubtless will serve as the basis of all future investigation. His interpretation of the "Christian symbols" on bronze and silver coins is especially noteworthy, for he concludes that these cannot be taken as proof of Constantine's conversion.*

**Patrick Bruun**

## *Conversion and the Coins*

Research into Constantinian history is most usually employed to shed some light on the controversial question concerning the conversion of Constantine and the emperor's attitude towards the Church. To neglect this aspect here would be almost heretical.

Yet the coins give no positive evidence of any conversion, but only of a gradually changing attitude towards the old gods. The break with tetrarchic conservatism marked by the adoption of the Sol imagery is more of a claim to supremacy and a challenge of Jupiter's ideological domination than a profession of faith. So too the disappearance of Sol witnesses yet another step on the path to divine rulership rather than the banishment of the image of the main opponent of the Christian God. The vota coinages exalted the emperor and his House, and they yielded only when the heaven-inspired ruler vested with the diadem had replaced the traditional effigy of the Roman emperor.

The arguments have been centred around Constantine's heavenly vision and the victorious sign of the Milvian Bridge. The vision, whether fictitious or real, was no doubt of paramount importance for the building up of the Constantinian legend. Thus, regardless of its historicity, it assumes historical importance. The sign, at the moment of its creation, was ambiguous. In essence it was a monogram

---

*This selection is taken from *Roman Imperial Coinage*, vol. VII, by Dr. Patrick Bruun, published by Spink and Son, London (1966), pp. 61–64. Footnotes omitted. The pages reproduced here give a summary of analyses carried out in *Roman Imperial Coinage* and in studies referred to in the footnotes appearing in the original of these pages but omitted here.

composed of the Greek letters X P, and, while the monogrammatic combination of these two letters was by no means unusual in pre-Constantinian times, the occurrence of X P with a clearly Christian significance is exceedingly rare. At least Greek-speaking Christians were therefore probably in a position to realize the possibilities of interpretation when confronted with the new sign. To others ☧ or ✝ was a powerful heavenly sign, in the eyes of some possibly recalling Sun worship and the Mithras cult, to others suggesting the mystic Eygptian *ankh.*

Quite apart from the personal religious conviction of Constantine, the sign was diffused as the victorious symbol of the emperor. The distinctly Christian character of ☧ represents a later stage of development. In so far as religious tolerance implied a victory for Christianity, intrinsically connected with Constantine and the battle of the Milvian Bridge, the sign became a symbol of that victory and finally assumed an exclusively Christian significance.

As a symbol of Constantinian victory the ☧ (at times graphically drawn ✳) appears on the coins, most frequently in a subordinate position, employed as a mark of issue or imperial rank. In this capacity the mark must have been accepted (and chosen) by the *procurator monetae;* in one instance the responsibility may have been even higher up, with the *rationalis summarum,* but still very far from emperor and court and *comes sacrarum largitionum.*[1] Certain others signs interpreted as Christian were employed in the same capacity, as mint-marks; in all these cases the responsibility was the procurator's, and the Christian character of the signs

was extremely dubious, to say the least, if we except the very unusual cross used as a serial mark at Aquileia in the last years of Constantine's reign.

Two details merit closer inspection — the coins with the new bowl-shaped, high-crested Constantinian helmet, and the Constantinopolitan type SPES PVBLIC showing the labarum piercing a dragon (a serpent). The former is a case of the ☧ decorating the helmet and thus being an integral part of the sign of the potency inherent in the imperial portrait. The helmet, occurring on the silver SALVS REIPVBLICAE multiples of Ticinum and on the bronzes of the type *Victoriae laetae princ perp,* has been a recurring theme in the prolific work of that great numismatist Andreas Alföldi. A detailed presentation and refutation of his theories on this particular point would take us too far. Let it suffice to state that the "Christograms" on the helmets of the bronze coins, seen in profile, are quite exceptional and must be considered to be engraver's slips. Of all the signs Alföldi purported to find on the helmet, including the cross-like marks on the bowl on either side of the cross-bar, only the ☧ on the cross-bar can have any symbolic significance. Yet these ☧ signs occur in the issues of Siscia alone exclusively in the third of five series and, as already stated, on a few individual specimens only. It is therefore impossible that all the other signs represent degenerated Christograms, and this applies to the Siscian coins as well as to the coins of all other pertinent mints.

The silver multiples with their facing portraits represent an altogether different case. The ☧ is here set in a badge just below the root of the crest. The official character of the badge has recently been demonstrated in a convincing manner. No doubt, therefore, persists about the meaning of the new emblem: the emperor had

---

[1] These were the finance ministers, appointed by the emperor, who controlled mines and the mints.— Ed.

adopted his own victorious sign as an emblem of power.

The elaborate bust of the silver multiple has yet another interesting trait. The emperor holds a horse by the bridle with his right hand, and a shield on his left arm. Across the left shoulder he carries an object, described by Alföldi as a cross-sceptre, and accordingly regarded as a new Christian sign of power. It has now been established that the globe surmounting the so-called sceptre is nothing but the globular end of a reversed spear, such as is frequently seen on the coins, though rarely so minutely executed. The cross-bar of the sceptre should consequently be identified with a cross-section of the disk separating the globular end from the shaft proper. It would, indeed, have been curious to find a one-dimensional cross-bar supporting a two-dimensional globe.

The character of the *Salus reipublicae* obverse is thus satisfactorily explained, but there remains the corollary of the *Constantinopolis* obverses, showing Constantinople holding an object usually described as a sceptre because of its frequent resemblance to the so-called cross-sceptre. An analysis of the relevant coins suggests that the basic design includes a cross-bar. We can hardly doubt that this actually corresponds to the disk, just as on the silver multiple. Nevertheless, it is possible that the unusual execution of the silver medallion created an iconographic precedent, subsequently adopted for the *Constantinopolis* obverses.

The problem of the labarum piercing the dragon on the Constantinopolitan *Spes public* bronzes remains. Here again we find the vexillum, the standard of the emperor with his personal victorious sign on top, piercing his foremost foe, the internal enemy Licinius, symbolized by the dragon (or serpent).

Such is the tale of the coins. Christian symbolism has no place on the coins of Constantine, but, again, this does not necessarily tell us anything of the personal conviction of the emperor or give any clues as to his religious policy. We have noted the original ambiguity of the signs ☧ and ☩. Other signs, artistic representations and expressions may appear to be equally vague, hovering between paganism and Christianity. This is the natural state of affairs. There was no independently Christian artistic tradition. The Christian ideas now about to conquer the State had to employ old means to express new conceptions. Only gradually does the new pictorial language find its *métier,* and Constantinian history in a decisive way affect the future development. The victor is the official interpreter of history, and Christianity was to be the true victor of the Milvian Bridge and Chrysopolis. Thus Constantine's victorious sign, his personal standard, his helmet, his seeming cross-sceptre and the aura around his head were adopted by posterity as Christian symbols, Christian signs of power. The Augustan age, similarly, had exerted a dominating influence on the first centuries of the Roman Empire.

In the following selection RAMSAY MacMULLEN (b. 1928), professor of ancient history at Yale University, examines Constantine's vision and conversion in the context of fourth-century supernaturalism. As he points out, this was a period in which magic spells, incantations, and the like were thought to influence human action, and the most mundane occurrences were commonly explained in providential terms. In this environment, he suggests, it is not surprising that Constantine's experience at the Milvian Bridge was readily attributed to the benevolent intervention of a deity.*

Ramsay MacMullen

# Constantine and the Miraculous

One day saw Constantine a pagan, the next a Christian, all thanks to the vision of a refulgent cross burning above him. So runs the familiar story. But told in this manner, apparently lacking precedent or preparation or context, it challenges belief. Readers of Lactantius or Eusebius, more alert than those hitsorians themselves to the course of the events they trace, now point to many gradual steps by which the emperor actually changed his public adherence from old gods to new, bringing his empire with him. They point, moreover, to bridges of thought touching both paganism and Christianity by which men like Constantine could pass from one to the other without need violently to repudiate their earlier worships and without need of any miraculous or magical act from on high. In fact, acts of the latter sort themselves constituted a part of the bridge, and it is on them that the following pages will focus, with citation of as many authors of Constantine's whole lifetime as are pertinent. It is the spread and prevalence of ideas as much as their content that will concern us.

Constantine's cross, a model for several similar appearances later, evidently served the credulity of his times. Such a sign was to meet the Caesar Gallus at Antioch as he entered that city, "a cruciform pillar in the sky" visible to other spectators as well, and Constantius,[1] about

_____
[1] Constantius II, sole emperor 350–361.—Ed.

*Reprinted from Ramsay MacMullen, "Constantine and the Miraculous," *Greek, Roman and Byzantine Studies,* 9 (Duke University, 1968), 81–96, by permission of the author and the editors. Footnotes omitted.

to engage Magnentius in battle, was not only favored with the same miracle but the citizens of Jerusalem attested its simultaneous appearance in the East stretching from the Mount of Calvary as far as the Mount of Olives. To the pious emperor it brought victory, to Magnentius' troops terror, "because they worshipped demons."

Constantius' reign witnessed divine intervention on another front. Persians beleaguered Nisibis where, among the Roman defenders, the holy bishop James of Antioch sent up his entreaties for aid. In response a kingly figure ablaze with crown and purple robe stood out upon the battlements, in whom the Persians recognized the Christian God; and James, himself mounting next, cursed the enemy with hordes of gnats that attacked their horses and elephants, putting them all to flight. Plagues of stinging insects first fell at Moses' command on Egypt; more recent ones were known, attributed to divine anger, and the efficacy of prayer in battle was to recur also, as that which Theodosius uttered against Eugenius in 393, raising a mighty wind to blow the rebels' missiles back in their faces. In so many ways did the incidents at Nisibis build on themes which were the common property of Christians in that period, just as the story of Theodosius and Eugenius likewise could be counted on to remind its audience of a storm they all had heard about, the famous storm that saved the "Thundering Legion" under Marcus Aurelius when Germans and Sarmatians beset his army. For this miracle, in an altogether typical contention over events certainly historical (confirmed by Marcus Aurelius' sculptured Column as well as by his coin-issues), Christians credited their fellows, pagans turned for explanation to a wonder-worker of the time, one Julianus, or to an Egyptian

magician, Arnouphis, who "had summoned by enchantment certain demons, above all, Hermes the aerial, and through them had brought on the rainstorm."

But the figure of God Himself threatening Persians from the walls of Nisibis was more spectacular than these deluges and winds. Parallels are thus correspondingly rare. An early glimpse into the popular mind is offered by the *Acta Andreae* of the last quarter of the second century. It relates how the saint and his companions, "proceeding through Thrace, met a troop of armed men who made as if to fall on them. Andrew made the sign of the cross against them and prayed that they might be made powerless. A bright angel touched their swords and they all fell down." Eusebius later (*Vita Const.* 2.6) tells of detachments of Constantine's forces—where none really were, hence miraculous troops—marching through eastern cities on the eve of the battle with Licinius, sent "by a divine and superior power." Two other examples are found in Socrates' *Ecclesiastical History* (6.6, 7.18): "multitudes of angels . . . like armored soldiers of great stature" who vanquished Gainas; "the angels from God [who] appeared to people in Bithynia . . . [and] said they were sent as arbiters over the war." Better yet is the "demonic apparition" drawn by Eusebius from Josephus (*HE* 3.8.5; Joseph. *BJ* 290f): "before sunset in the air throughout the country chariots and regiments [were seen] flying through the clouds and encircling the cities." Among pagan writers, on the other hand, such miraculous beings play a smaller part. A woman of gigantic form turns up in Dio Cassius' pages almost as a genre-figure. Dio asserts his personal belief in her, whether in the scene of Drusus crossing the Elbe or upon the crisis of Macrinus' reign in 217. Herodian (8.3.8) goes further. The occasion as he describes it is the closing in of Maximinus' legions on Aquileia in 238. To the townspeople "certain oracles were given that the deity of the region would grant them victory. They call him Belis, worship him mightily, and identify him with Apollo. His image, some of Maximinus' troops reported, often appeared in the skies fighting in defense of the city"—which returns us to Constantine.

For that susceptible emperor had *two* visions, not only of a cross but (somewhat less well known if hardly less debated by scholars) an earlier one of Apollo. It came to him on his way south from the Rhine to defeat Maximian in Marseilles. He turned aside en route to a temple of Apollo, "whom you saw, I believe, O Constantine—your Apollo accompanied by Victory holding out laurelled crowns to you each of which brought the presage of thirty years [of rule] . . . And yet why do I say, 'I believe'? You saw and you recognized him in the form to which . . . the reigns of all the world were destined" (*Paneg. vet.* 7[6].21.3–5). "You saw," presumably as others by the score had seen some deity invoked by magic or freely offering himself to them, and as, in later embroidered versions, Constantine's second vision was explained to him personally by Christ. Superhuman beings, then, who revealed themselves to their worshippers before armed conflict or whose agents or powers were exerted for the battalions of the pious were a feature of pagan as of Christian mythology in the third and fourth centuries; and no better illustration of this common ground can be found than the spiritual career of Constantine between 310 and 312.

His panegyrists noted elements throughout his rise and reign beyond mere mortal reach. Sometimes such notice was blurred and vague, for example, in the emphasis of Nazarius on Constantine's "celestial favor," the victims "divinely granted to your arms," "the divinity accustomed to forward your undertakings," and so forth—expressions shading off into ambiguities common among both pagan and Christian writers. . . . More often the notices of Constantine's protector are explicit, as in the paragraphs devoted by Eusebius (*HE* 10.8.6–9) to proving his hero God's representative on earth.

With Constantine, indeed, the sense that men, especially leaders of state, acted as servants of some supernal purpose and thus played their roles under its direction, took firm hold on the minds of contemporaries, as was bound to come about from the ascendance of so historically oriented a religion as Christianity. . . .

Upon his conversion, Constantine entered into this whole heritage of beliefs— the belief that a pious people would receive divine protection, that their ruler ruled according to divine plan, and that God directly or through his angels could be expected to intercede in their behalf at crucial moments. Thus, to Maxentius' fateful collision with Constantine at the Milvian Bridge, "God Himself as with chains dragged the tyrant far away from the [safety of Rome's] gates."

The question how pagans looked on the position of the Roman emperors *vis à vis* the gods has been surprisingly little studied, despite a mass of material. It is fortunately tangential to our purpose. Two points only need be made. In the first place, the idea of national guardian angels, though familiar to writers like Celsus, Porphyry, Iamblichus and Julian, did not lead to a concept of supernatural intervention in terrestrial happenings; nor (in the second place) did the concept of the ruler favored or even chosen by the gods develop further into the expectation that they would miraculously succor him in the hour of national crisis. Not until challenged by Christianity did pagans give any sharpness to their claims that their own piety could secure the safety of the state or the victorious outcome of a campaign. In Constantine's lifetime, a change can be seen. In the transition to an era of far more intense and vaunting religious propaganda, the battle of the Milvian Bridge was critical. Thereafter, through the conflicts involving Licinius and Maximin and so to the historic conversion of Clovis in the following century, battle was determined, so men said, by divine judgement.

But to return to Constantine: newly converted, he advanced into Italy in 312. His decision to make war, his march, his feelings and motives, all receive a characteristic treatment at the hands of spokesmen for the Church. But they make the meaning of the march clearer by their description of his opponent, who, we are told, huddles in Rome gripped by terror, vice and superstition, dupe to countless religious charlatans, petitioner to countless vain spirits, convert to such revolting measures as the tearing of unborn babes from the womb for use in prognostic sacrifices. Though the picture of his *superstitiosa maleficia* [superstitious crimes] is a compendium of commonplaces, it sets the stage for the dramatic collision of the two religious worlds. This is the significance felt by historians of the battle of the Milvian Bridge. The old world failed, whatever devices were desperately attempted; the new conquered, in the first campaign of a century's religious strife.

This strife was carried on not merely by men but by supernatural forces, too. If the Sibylline books, demons, priests and the rest deceived Maxentius, it is at any rate

they who fought as well as he; and their enemy was not the western emperor but the Savior's sign. The sign may then have been the *chrisma* and only in later battles the cross; more likely, at the Milvian Bridge as throughout the rest of Constantine's career, the cross. Its cherished use in war, its invariable efficacy whether on armor or on the *labarum* and whether to protect emperor or humble standard-bearer, set it above all other forces, yet the relation between the *labarum* and the traditional Roman *vexillum* is obvious, while the painting of a declaratory or magical device on the shields of one's troops had earlier close parallels. Even the tales of the defensive properties of the cross in combat are matched by the inscriptions found on pieces of military equipment from the centuries just before Constantine, reading "Luck to the bearer" or "Best and Greatest, save the corps of all our soldiers"; Mars or Victory might be depicted on armor. Such evidence shows us the well-worn paths that Constantine trod when, according to the ancient arts of apotropaic magic though with a different device, he put the insignia of Christianity in the hands of his followers.

On the history of those insignia there is no need for much discussion. Their potency to tear demons from their lairs in statues, to uproot them from unhappy maniacs, to drive them forever from shrines and temples to the accompaniment of their anguished howls and supplications—all this is attested in dozens of accounts of Christ's cross or name in the service of the faithful. So mighty was the weapon that Constantine aimed at Maxentius' weaker gods. But Constantine extended its use. His mother Helena sent him a piece of the true cross. "When he received it, confident that the city in which it was kept would be preserved forever, he hid it in a statue of himself standing in the so-called Forum of Constantine in Constantinople, on a large porphyry column"—thereby producing the Christian equivalent of those images of the pagan gods that, both earlier and later, deflected enemies' attacks. They guarded Nero against conspiracies, Ephesus against plagues, Athens against earthquakes, Rome against sedition.

Constantine's actions fitted the times. Apotropaic magic to ward off disease was on the increase. Lucky stones with mystic signs and spells on them grew more popular in the third and fourth centuries than ever before, evidently among both Christians and pagans, since the synods of Ancyra (under Constantine) and of Laodicea (between 341 and 381) spoke out against "those who foretell the future and follow the customs of the heathen, or introduce persons into their houses to find out magical remedies or to perform purifications," or against priests who "shall not be magicians or enchanters or astrologers or make so-called phylacteries [amulets] . . . and those who wear them we order to be expelled from the Church."

Eusebius tells the tale of Caesarea in Palestine where once lived the woman whom Christ cured of an issue of blood. At the gates of her house stood two statues which he himself had seen, one of a woman praying, the other of a man resembling Jesus. At the base of the latter grew a curious herb able to "cure diseases of all kinds." To this wonder we must add the power of the true cross that Helena discovered to heal the sick: thus, two illustrations of the workings of *Christus medicus,* in opposition especially to the authority enjoyed by Asclepius. But it was, after all, essential for the Church to present its founder as a God of deeds equal to the performances of pagan deities, since, particularly for a mass audience, proof

through miracles offered an infinitely more persuasive appeal than the type of argument carried on in written form. Simple people wanted simple proof of the superior ability of Christianity to do for them what older worships had always promised: that is, to defend them from the ills of this earth. The dreams granted at Asclepieia taught suppliants how to be healed. Could Christ or his holy men do as much? And if the answer was yes, in scores of wonders wrought especially by monks, there remained the more general affliction of epidemic disease. Throughout antiquity men attributed plagues to divine anger. A persistent conviction blamed their onset on the progress of Christianity and the resulting neglect of pagan cults. It was a heavy charge variously answered; but one response as it was ultimately framed in pious myth said that even in averting disease Christians had access to a more greatly beneficent power than pagan wonderworkers.

With a few exceptions—Eusebius was one—Christians, like pagans, acknowledged the supernatural origin of plagues, as they did of other bodily ills which they could not understand. Ailments afflicting (in grotesquely disgusting descriptions) especially the intestines and genitals marked the victim as the target of a god's, or of God's, wrath; the genre is well known and meets us most often in the heated religious atmosphere of the fourth century. Manic fits likewise called more for the exorcist than the doctor, and Christians claimed to possess the requisite skills more than their opponents. Palladius and Sozomen supply an abundance of case-histories. It was the same with other mysterious catastrophes: sterility of the fields, insect-pests, hail, drought, earthquakes, storms. Great winds, said Maximin Daia, were controlled by the gods, and could be turned on or off by their favor or displeasure. Jealous courtiers of Constantine accused the influential wise man Sopater of having "chained the winds" that were to bring the grain fleet to the capital; whereupon the emperor, evidently convinced that the man was actually capable of the necessary enchantments, executed him.

Believing that natural phenomena, from earthquakes to the wasting of the flesh, were in fact all supernatural, people of the later Empire saw in their afflictions a working out of divine conflicts on a terrestrial plane or stage. Pagans accused Christians of causing these conflicts and their resultant sufferings. In the Apologists the echoes of such accusations — *popularia verba* [popular sayings], said Arnobius — are plainly heard; individual instances of persecution breaking out in the train, and because of the typical interpretation, of droughts and earthquakes are fairly often recorded. It was thought that droughts and the like might be deliberately inflicted in response to invocation or upon people hateful to the gods, though it was still more usually argued that the protectors of cities and nations had been neglected, and had for this reason departed. The sum total of the later Empire's ill-fortunes could thus, to Zosimus, appear to follow from the abandonment of ancestral cults and rites. He singles out for his criticism the decision of Constantine not to hold the *ludi saeculares,*[2] in order that he may strike a blow at that hero of the Church.

Here, then, is another part of the background to the battle of the Milvian Bridge: terrestrial events of a striking, public character were thought to result from supernatural intercession whether

[2] The "secular games" theoretically were to be held every hundred years to celebrate the founding of the city of Rome. — Ed.

spontaneous or invoked. It was neither improper nor uncommon for Christians to give credence to happenings of this order, and it was frowned on only if it degenerated to the private practice of magic. Pagans of course enjoyed a wider latitude in superstition, without, however, any fundamentally different views.

To understand a further aspect of the collision between Maxentius and Constantine, some discussion of demons is needed. The term, in Greek or by adoption in Latin, had the broadest meaning. Pagan philosophers used it to designate, between the crass material of mankind and the etherial realm of pure intellect, the denizens of an intermediate world who served as agents and emissaries from the higher to the lower and (conducting the souls of the dead and the prayers of the living) from the lower to the higher. These denizens had ranks according to their insubstantiality and intellectuality, the purer ones sometimes called angels but often not differentiated under a separate category. They linked men to gods. Foreign as was most of this hierarchy of intermediaries to classical Greek thought, it can be seen developing in the second century and went virtually unquestioned in the later Empire. Its roots lay partly in a substratum of popular superstition, partly in Oriental religions. To mention only points of interest to our present purpose: it was demons who occasioned earthquakes, pests and so forth; they again who brought oracles from the gods and cured the sick; sometimes, too, harmed men when called on with the proper enchantments. Outstanding minds of late antiquity, Porphyry and Libanius, were quite sure that magic could be enlisted in the cause of personal vendettas — though the pure in spirit were beyond the reach of demons. The more evil among demons longed to gorge themselves on sacrifices, to experience sexual intercourse vicariously through the bodies of the possessed, and to deceive with false revelations. Sometimes demons dwelt in cult images; they would not appear in impure places and shunned a hostile presence. To different ones among them different temples, even different zones or, more specifically, nations and peoples, had been assigned for oversight, and they occasionally took visible human shape to meddle directly in the course of events. According to a particularly common conviction, the Devil—$\delta$ μισόκαλος [the one who hates the good; that is, the Evil One]—or his agents continually worked against the progress or unity of the Church by spreading false doctrines, libels, suspicions against Christians, and the like. Infected with these diabolical errors, heretics and persecutors became mere instruments of a wickedness from beyond.

Strange views, perhaps. But as a darkness of irrationality thickened over the declining centuries of the Roman empire, superstition blacked out the clearer lights of religion, wizards masqueraded as philosophers, and the fears of the masses took hold on those who passed for educated and enlightened. From the same world, reflecting of necessity the same ideas because surrounded by them in all social classes, rose the leaders of the Church. Thus all of the opinions about demons (by that specific term, *daemon* or δαίμων) just now reviewed as representing the consensus of pagan thought also reigned as orthodoxy among Christians like Origen, Lactantius, Eusebius, Basil, Gregory and many others, though with this major difference, that the intermediaries between mortal and divine were conceived of as good and bad angels, the latter being equated (under the name "demons") with the pagan gods. It hardly occurred to Christians to deny the whole infinite list of the older deities; only as many as possible were traced back to men as heroes, according to the traditional teachings of Euhemerism, while those that could not be talked out of existence in this fashion were left to deceive men with false visions, false cures, false oracles and insidious intrusions of shameful lust. This last trial especially will be recalled by readers of Athanasius' *Vita S. Antoni*. Anthony declared himself the target of temptation by beautiful succubi some of whom, it is permissible to imagine, were simply pious peasant girls coming to venerate the saint. The mistake, at any rate, is once attested of a bishop of Constantius' time, spending the night at an inn. A woman entered in the dark, the bishop asked, "Who's there?" and hearing her voice concluded she was a demon in female form. "Straightway he called on Christ the Savior to help him." The instinctive assumption that unearthly forces were at work tells us much about the spirit of the age. . . .

The atmosphere of contentious comparison, the tendency to prove the superiority of one's faith by matching its miraculous powers with another's, emerged suddenly from books to the stage of real events in Constantine's lifetime. The conditions making this possible were all present. What was required was a conviction that powers accessible to men through invocation, and willing to intervene in tangible forms and happenings—moreover, powers potentially hostile to each other—filled the universe. It was necessary, too, that such a conviction should be held by the great mass of people, as was indeed the case. Our sketch so far, relying more on anecdotes than analysis, has been intended to reveal society shot through at all levels with the colors of a grosser superstition, with cruder expectations of the supernatural than one could find in the Empire at its height.

The consequences appeared first in the origins of the Great Persecution, of which

Constantine, incidentally, was a witness. As Diocletian was assisting in the ceremony of *extispicium*,[3] Christians in his retinue crossed themselves, "by which act the demons were put to flight and the ritual disturbed." The chief priest explained why the entrails refused to yield their prophetic message, whereupon the emperor flew into a rage at those guilty of the disturbance. The incident is well known; but not so often emphasized is the conception of demonic conflict that lay behind Lactantius' account: one superhuman power could drive away another, magic worked only in the absence of inimical forces. Evidence for those views has been gathered above. After Lactantius, Church historians multiplied imitations of the story, sometimes by retrojection: for example, "The teacher and arch-priest of Egyptian magicians persuaded him [Valerian] to get rid of them [Christians], bidding him kill and drive away the pure and holy men as being enemies and preventers of his foul and disgusting spells (for they are and were able, by being present and by watching and by simply breathing on them and speaking, to scatter the plots of baneful demons)." Until the end of Eusebius' century and even beyond, though with diminishing report, the noise of battle was to sound as it were contrapuntally between Christians and pagans on earth, and between their gods invisible in shrines, in the heavens, in the nether regions and in men's minds—a battle, however, in which the combatants struggled with identical weapons of attack and on the same field of ideas.

Men who controlled gods, great wonder-workers, launched their superhuman agents or allies against their rivals, in duels more fit for a Greek novella; yet they were recounted in sober prose. Witness the vision of a certain persecutor of pagan wise men, one Festus, in which he saw a former victim "throwing a noose around his [Festus'] neck and dragging him down to Hades . . . As he came out [of the temple in which the vision came to him], his feet slipped from under him and he fell on his back and lay speechless there. He was borne away immediately and died, and this seemed to be an outstanding work of Providence (πρόνοια)." We need change only the proportions of the story, from two individuals to two causes and armies, to have the prelude to the battle of the Milvian Bridge. On the one side is Constantine with his vision, his prayers, his divine support, his miraculous symbol borne before his troops; on the other is Maxentius busied with "certain unspeakable invocations to demons and deterrents of war," vain, as it turns out, and powerless against the mightier arsenal of Christianity.

How much in the scene can be credited? Were our whole basis of understanding the pages of Eusebius alone, we might, like Burckhardt a hundred years ago, replace the supernatural elements with others more easily acceptable to a modern mind. Anachronistic rationalism, however, only misleads; the interpretation suggested by more recent scholars, notably Alföldi, is surely right. In the light of the beliefs surveyed in the foregoing pages, we must suppose that Constantine's contemporaries (why not himself, then?) did in truth fear antagonistic wizardry, did put their faith in supernatural aid to be exerted visibly on the very field of battle, accepted without skepticism the powers claimed both for Maxentius' sacrifices and for the symbol of the cross, and looked on the whole struggle of old against new religion as being greater than, but no different in kind from, the operation of magicians' spells and counter-spells.

---

[3] In which haruspices predicted the future through an examination of animal entrails.—Ed.

A. H. M. JONES (1904–1970), late professor of ancient
history and fellow of Jesus College, Cambridge
University, is author of the indispensable economic,
social, and administrative survey, *The Later Roman
Empire 284–602* (1964). In the selection printed here,
Jones, like Baynes, bases his interpretation of the
conversion on official documents, the most important
of which are reproduced in translation. His most novel
contribution to the debate is the suggestion that the
vision "seen" by Constantine may have been a rare form
of the "halo phenomenon."*

A. H. M. Jones

# *The Fortuitous Event*

That Constantine was in some sense
converted to Christianity in the year 312
there is no manner of doubt. But at this
point agreement ceases. The debate still
goes on whether his conversion was a matter of policy or of religious conviction,
and in the latter alternative what brought
about his change of heart, and finally
whether he became a full Christian or
whether he passed through a stage when
he regarded Christianity as one of many
forms in which the Supreme Power could
be worshipped. On the first question no
historian who understands the mood of
the age in which Constantine lived can
entertain any serious doubts. To be a
rationalist in that age Constantine would
have been an intellectual prodigy, and he
was, in fact, so far as we can discern him,
a simple-minded man. And even if, by
some freak of nature, he had been a sceptical freethinker, he would not on any
rational calculation of his interest have
chosen to profess Christianity. The Christians were a tiny minority of the population, and they belonged for the most part
to the classes of the population who were
politically and socially of least importance, the middle and lower classes of the
towns. The senatorial aristocracy of Rome
were pagan almost to a man; the higher
grades of the civil service were mainly
pagan; and above all the army officers
and men, were predominantly pagan. The
goodwill of the Christians was hardly
worth gaining, and for what it was worth

*Reprinted with permission of The Macmillan Company and the English Universities Press Limited
from *Constantine and the Conversion of Europe* by A. H. M. Jones, pp. 73–90. First printed in 1948. Copyright
© 1962 by A. H. M. Jones.

it could be gained by merely granting them toleration. On the other questions there is doubt, for the evidence is tangled and in parts contradictory. It will be best first to set out the external facts—Constantine's actions, his official pronouncements and the public utterances of his contemporaries.

Long before the defeat of Maxentius, Constantine had favoured the Christians: he had granted them full toleration immediately upon his accession to power. But no ancient author claims that he was during that period a Christian, and the orators who from time to time delivered panegyrics before him had no hesitation in representing the pagan gods as his protectors. As late as July 311, Eumenius, in giving thanks for a remission of taxes on behalf of Autun, could say without offence, "Our gods have created you emperor for our special benefit," and compare Constantine's generosity with that of "Earth, the author of crops, and Jupiter, the governor of the winds."

Directly after the capture of Rome, Constantine went beyond toleration for the Christians. We possess three letters which he wrote during the winter of 312–13, one to Caecilian, bishop of Carthage, and two to Anullinus, proconsul of Africa. As the earliest evidence of Constantine's new attitude to the Church, they are worth quoting in full. The first runs:

Constantine Augustus to Caecilian, bishop of Carthage.

Whereas I have decided that in all the provinces, the Africas, the Numidias and the Mauretanias, provision should be made for expenses to stated numbers of the servants of the lawful and most holy Catholic Church, I have written to Ursus, the accountant of Africa, instructing him to cause to be paid to your reverence 3,000 folles. You will therefore, upon receipt of the aforesaid sum, order the money to be distributed to all the previously mentioned persons in accordance with the list which has been sent to you by Hosius. If you discover that it is inadequate in order to fulfil my wishes in this matter towards all of them, you must without hesitation demand whatever you discover is needed from Heraclides, the intendant of our domains. For I have ordered him personally to cause to be paid without any delay any sums which your reverence may demand from him. And since I have heard that certain persons of turbulent character wish to distract the people of the most holy Catholic Church by some base pretence, you must know that I have given such orders personally to Anullinus the proconsul and also to Patricius, deputy of the prefects, that among all their other business they will devote especial attention to this matter, and will not submit to seeing anything of the kind happen. Accordingly, if you should observe any such persons persisting in their insane designs, approach the above-mentioned officials without any hesitation, and refer the matter to them, so that they may deal with them as I ordered them personally. May the divinity of the great God preserve you for many years.

By this letter Constantine embarks on a new policy of subsidising the Christian Church from public funds; he no longer merely tolerates, but actively favours the Church. It is noteworthy, too, that he is already aware of the schism whereby the African Church was rent, and confines his favours to the side which he has been informed is the true Catholic Church. The source of his information is also revealed —the Spanish bishop, Hosius of Corduba. This is highly significant; for its suggests that Constantine had a Christian bishop at his court before he embarked on the Italian campaign.

Constantine's first letter to Anullinus runs as follows:

Greetings, our dearest Anullinus. It is the nature of our love of good that we are not merely not reluctant, but that we even wish to restore whatever belongs to others by right, dearest Anullinus. We therefore wish that when you receive this letter you shall immediately cause to be restored to the churches any of the property belonging to the Catholic Church of the Christians in the several cities or in other places, and now held either by private citizens or by any other persons. For we have decided that whatever the same churches previously held shall be restored to their ownership. Since therefore your devotion observes that the tenor of this our command is clear, take steps that gardens, houses, and all other property of the same churches are forthwith restored to them, so that we may hear that you have rendered the most careful obedience to this our command. Farewell, our dearest and most beloved Anullinus.

In this letter Constantine is merely righting the wrongs inflicted by the persecutions. The second is more significant.

Greetings, our dearest Anullinus. Whereas from many considerations it appears that the annulment of the worship in which the highest reverence of the most holy heavenly power is maintained has brought the greatest dangers upon the commonwealth, and the lawful revival and protection of this same worship has caused the greatest good fortune to the Roman name and exceptional prosperity to all the affairs of men, the divine beneficence affording this, it has been decided that those men who in due holiness and the observance of this law offer their personal services to the ministry of the divine worship shall receive the due reward of their labours, dearest Anullinus. Accordingly I desire that those who within the province entrusted to you provide personal service to this holy worship in the Catholic Church over which Caecilian presides, who are commonly called 'clerics,' shall be kept immune from all public burdens of any kind whatever, so that they may not be diverted by any sacrilegious error or slip from the service which is owed to the Divinity, but may rather without any disturbance serve their own law, since their conduct of the greatest worship towards the Divinity will in my opinion bring

immeasurable benefit to the commonwealth. Farewell, our dearest and most beloved Anullinus.

This letter reveals something quite new in Constantine's thought. The worship offered by the Christian Church to the Divinity is to his mind of vital importance to the well-being of the empire; the persecution of the Church has brought the empire into peril, its restoration and maintenance has brought it good fortune. It is clear that Constantine regarded Christianity, not merely as a permissible and a laudable cult, but as the form of worship most acceptable to the supreme power in whose hands the destinies of the empire lay.

In February 313 Constantine and Licinius met at Milan. The marriage of Licinius and Constantia, Constantine's half-sister, which had been arranged two years before, was celebrated, and a common policy was agreed between the two emperors. The conference was suddenly interrupted by the news that Maximin had crossed the Bosphorus.

Maximin had no doubt expected that his ally Maxentius would put up a stubborn resistance to Constantine's attack, and that Licinus would have been drawn into the struggle: his plan had been to attack Licinius in the rear while he was thus engaged. Constantine's lightning campaign and Maxentius' sudden collapse had thrown his plans out of joint, but he was convinced that he would be the next victim of Licinius and Constantine. He could gain nothing by delay: his only chance of survival was to strike first. The majority of Licinius' troops had been withdrawn to the Italian frontier: he had 70,000 men mobilised in Bithynia. Licinius was a parsimonious paymaster, whereas he was lavish with his soldiers. A quick victory might provoke a mass desertion of Licinius by his troops.

The garrison of Byzantium resisted Maximin's blandishments and assaults for eleven days. On their surrender Maximin marched on Heraclea, which delayed him a few more days, and then he advanced eighteen miles to the first post-station along the road leading westwards to Hadrianople. Here he was forced to halt, for during the few weeks that he had been held up at Byzantium and Heraclea, Licinius had been informed of his attack, and had raced from Milan to Hadrianople, picking up troops by the way, and now occupied the next post-station, eighteen miles ahead, with a force of 30,000 men.

On 30th April Maximin deployed his troops for battle. Licinius, despite the fact that he was outnumbered by more than two to one, accepted the challenge. For he did not rely on human resources alone. As his troops came into line they grounded their shields, removed their helmets, and raising their arms to the sky, recited in unison, their officers dictating the words, the following prayer:

Highest God, we beseech thee, Holy God, we beseech thee; to Thee we commend all justice, to Thee we commend our safety, to Thee we commend our Empire. Through Thee we live, through Thee we are victorious and fortunate. Highest, Holy God, hear our prayers: we stretch out our arms to Thee; hear us, Holy, Highest God.

The battle was swift and decisive. Maximin, flinging off his imperial robes and disguising himself as a slave, fled posthaste for the straits. He reached them in twenty-four hours, and in another twenty-four was back in Nicomedia. Then, having picked up his family and his ministers, he made for Cappadocia, where he resumed his imperial robes and collected troops for a second stand.

Licinius entered Nicomedia in triumph, and on 15th June issued the following constitution to the governor of Bithynia:

When both I, Constantine Augustus and also I, Licinius Augustus, had happily met at Milan, and debated all measures which pertained to the interest and security of the State, we considered that among other matters which we saw would benefit a large number of persons, the very first that required regulation was that wherein was comprised respect for the Divinity: that we should give both to the Christians and to all others free power of following whatever religion each individual wished, in order that whatever Divinity there be in the heavenly seat can be appeased and propitious to us and to all who are placed under our rule. Accordingly we considered that this policy was to be prudently and rightly adopted, so that we thought that no person should be denied the opportunity of devoting himself either to the cult of the Christians or to whatever religion he himself felt most suitable for himself: in order that the Highest Divinity, whose worship we practise with free hearts, can afford to us in all things His wonted favour and kindness. Accordingly your Excellency must know that we have resolved that all kinds of conditions, which in previous communications addressed to your office appeared to apply to the case of the Christians, are to be removed, and that now everyone of those who have the same desire for observing the religion of the Christians is freely and unconditionally, without any interference or molestation, to hasten to observe it. We thought it proper to explain this very fully to your Excellency, that you might know that we have given to the same Christians free and absolute liberty to practise their religion. While you see that we have granted this grace to them, your Excellency will understand that others also have for the peace of our reign been similarly granted free and open liberty for their religion or cult, so that every individual may have free power of pursuing what worship he chooses. This we have resolved that we may not appear to diminish any worship or any religion. In the case of the Christians, we have decided to make the following additional regulations.

There follow orders for restoring forthwith to the community of the Christians their places of worship and their other property, whether they were still in the possession of the Treasury or had been sold or granted to private persons: the purchasers or grantees being promised ultimate compensation from the Treasury. "So it will come about that, as has been explained above, the Divine favour towards us, which we have experienced in such great events, will prosperously continue for all time, to our success and the public happiness."

Maximin must have already felt some qualms about his anti-Christian policy, for in the winter of 312–13 he had issued a constitution relaxing the persecution. This document opens with a curiously disingenuous historical preamble. Diocletian and Maximian, Maximin asserted, had very properly, seeing the worship of the gods neglected owing to the large numbers of persons who had adopted the Christian faith, endeavoured by disciplinary measures to recall the backsliders to the religion of the immortal gods. But he himself on his accession, in view of the large number of potentially useful citizens who were being driven from their homes by the authorities, had, he claimed, reversed this policy, and instructed his governors not to use violence, but to win over Christians by persuasion. Then Nicomedia, followed by other cities, had petitioned him to expel the Christinas from their territories, and he had ultimately felt obliged to accede to their petitions. Nevertheless, he confirms his previous orders that no Christian is to suffer violence or molestation by the officials, but only to be encouraged by persuasion to

return to the worship of the gods. Eusebius attributed this edict to pressure from Constantine and Licinius, but it was issued before they had met at Milan, and it was probably due to doubts that had arisen in Maximin's own mind. In 312 he had been defeated by the Christian King of Armenia, and in the following winter his dominions had been ravaged by famine and by an outburst of plague. Maximin may have felt that the God Whom the Christians worshipped was a dangerous enemy.

His defeat by Licinius left no room for doubt, and he now hastily issued an edict granting full liberty of worship to the Christians and restoring to them their confiscated churches and property. But this belated repentance did not profit him. As Licinius advanced swiftly from Nicomedia, Maximin withdrew through the Cilician gates to Tarsus: at the gates he might hope to hold up Licinius long enough to mobilise his forces from the Oriental diocese. But Licinius' troops quickly forced the pass and Maximin committed suicide.

From these events it is possible to reconstruct what had passed at Milan. Constantine and Licinius had agreed on a common policy towards the Christians: the property of the Church was to be restored and full and untrammelled liberty of worship permitted. Licinius' edict bears signs, in its laborious insistence that both Christians and others were to enjoy toleration, of being a compromise, and there can be little doubt in which direction either emperor was pulling. Constantine had already in his own dominions gone further than mere resitution and toleration: it must then have been Licinius who insisted on a strict impartiality.

It would also appear that Constantine had urged Licinius, in his forthcoming campaign against Maximin, to place his armies under the protection of that heavenly power which had granted his own armies victory over Maxentius. This advice Licinius apparently accepted with reservation. He did not adopt the sign under which Constantine's men had fought, and he drafted a form of prayer which, while it should be acceptable to the heavenly power, could give no offence to any other god.

We possess two works written during these years by Christians, one in Latin in the dominions of Constantine, the other in Greek in those of Licinius. Lactantius, the author of the Latin treatise, *On the Deaths of the Persecutors,* had, after Maxentius' fall, returned to the West to be appointed tutor to Constantine's eldest son Crispus. The Greek work is the ninth book of the *Church History* of Eusebius, bishop of Caesarea. This great work had originally been planned in eight books to end with the recantation of Galerius in 311. When Maximin renewed the persecution, only to be defeated and perish after a vain recantation of his errors, Eusebius added another book to his history. He was later, after the persecution and fall of Licinius, to add a tenth book, and to revise what he had said about Licinius in the ninth, but the revision was so superficial that the original can easily be reconstructed.

In both these works Constantine and Licinius are jointly acclaimed as champions of Christianity against persecutors. Reading them, one would infer that Licinius was as much a Christian as Constantine. Lactantius asserts that the prayer with which Licinius opened battle against Maximin was dictated to him in a dream by an angel of God, just as he declares that Constantine was instructed in a dream to paint the mysterious monogram on his soldiers' shields before the battle of the Milvian Bridge. Eusebius speaks of "the champions of peace and piety, Constantine and Licinius," and concludes his book with the triumphant sentence, "So when the impious had been purged away, the sovereignty that was theirs by right was preserved unshaken and ungrudged to Constantine and Licinius alone: they first of all purged away enmity to God from their lives, and recognising the blessings that God had bestowed upon them, demonstrated their love of virtue and of God, their piety and gratitude to the Divinity, by their legislation on behalf of the Christians." In a sermon which he preached at Tyre he went yet further, declaring that "now, as never before in history, the emperors, who are above all men, acknowledging the honour they have received from Him, spit in the faces of lifeless idols and trample underfoot the lawless laws of demons, laugh at the old traditional falsehoods, and acknowledge the one God alone as the benefactor of themselves and all men, and confess Christ as the Son of God and King of all."

The inference of the Christians that Licinius was a Christian was proved by subsequent events to be false. Can one say at this date that they were right in drawing the same conclusion about Constantine?

Constantine's pagan subjects have left little record of what they conceived his religious position to be, but some significant hints of their attitude have survived. The Senate, in order to celebrate Constantine's victory, erected a triumphal arch. The arch still stands and its inscription runs: "To the Emperor Caesar Flavius Constantine, the Greatest, the Pious, the Fortunate, Augustus, because by the prompting of the Divinity and the greatness of his soul, he with his forces avenged the commonwealth with just arms both on the tyrant and on all his faction, the Senate and people of Rome dedicated this triumphal arch." We cannot tell who composed this inscription: it must have been approved by the Emperor, but it may well have been drafted by the Senate. If so, the vague allusion to a nameless Divinity indicates that the Senators believed that any mention of the immortal gods would be offensive to the Emperor. In other words, they must have believed him to be a Christian, for no other sect or creed was intolerant of the gods.

The same conclusion is to be drawn from the panegyric which a Gallic rhetorician addressed to him, when, after the conference of Milan, he had moved to Trèves to inspect the Rhine frontier. The speech is naturally devoted to Constantine's victory over Maxentius. The orator marvels at the Emperor's boldness in attacking, unsupported by his colleagues, the tyrant who had defied the armies of Severus and Galerius. He rebukes him for his rashness in having left three-quarters of his troops to guard the Rhine frontier, and ignoring the protests of his generals, attacked 100,000 men with a bare quarter of his forces. What, he asks, was the source of the Emperor's confidence? "Surely," he replies, "you have some secret communion, Constantine, with that divine mind, which, delegating our care to lesser gods, deigns to reveal itself to you alone." This passage is the only mention of gods in the plural in the whole speech, and even here they are carefully dissociated from the Emperor. The Divine power which watches over Constantine is described in studiously vague terms; indeed, the peroration of the speech is a masterpiece of ambiguity. "Wherefore we pray thee, O highest creator of the world, whose names are as many as thou has willed that there be tongues of men—for what thou thyself wishest to be called, we cannot know—whether there be in thee

some divine power or intelligence, which being infused throughout the universe, thou art mingled in every element, and dost move of thine own self without the impulsion of any external force; or whether there be some power above every heaven, whereby thou lookest down upon thy handiwork from some higher peak of nature; to thee I say we pray, that thou mayest preserve this our Emperor for all ages." The passage is eloquent of the embarrassment of the pagan orator, forced to avoid all mention of the immortal gods, but averse from sullying his lips with any allusion to the God of the Christians.

It would appear that Constantine was regarded as a Christian by both his Christian and his pagan subjects from the time that he entered Rome. And this conclusion was natural, since Constantine had not only granted liberty of worship to the Christians and restored their confiscated property to the churches, but had subsidised the clergy and granted them immunities, and had in so doing expressed his conviction that the proper conduct of the Christian cult was of vital import to the prosperity and security of the empire. He had, moreover, painted on the shields of his soldiers a symbol which, though new and apparently of his own invention, could be interpreted as a monogram of Christ. And he had soon after his victory startlingly proclaimed his allegiance to the Cross. In a public place in Rome he had caused to be erected a statue of himself, holding in his right hand a cross, with this inscription (if Eusebius has correctly translated it) below: "By this sign of salvation, the true mark of valour, I saved your city and freed it from the yoke of the tyrant, and moreover having freed the senate and people of Rome, restored them to their ancient honour and glory." Against all this evidence is to be set the imperial coinage. The types and legends of the coinage, which were frequently changed from year to year, were a recognised vehicle of imperial propaganda. Nothing would have been easier than to eliminate from them all allusion to the pagan gods; for while it was common to place upon the coins representations of the gods, there were many religiously neutral types which were equally commonly used, celebrating the prosperity of the age, the valour of the armies, the concord of the emperors, peace, victory or plenty. Even if Constantine had hesitated to offend the great majority of his subjects by placing distinctively Christian symbols on his coins, he could, without exciting any adverse comment, have eliminated representations of the pagan gods. Yet for the next five years the mints of Constantine's dominions continued to issue coins in honour of Hercules the Victorious, Mars the Preserver, Jupiter the Preserver, and above all the Unconquered Sun, the Companion of the Augusti: the last-named continues to be honoured at one mint down to 320. It is impossible to believe that these issues can have been continued for so many years merely by official inertia without exciting the notice of the Emperor. And at any rate one special issue must have received his positive approval. This is a set of magnificent gold medallions struck to celebrate the meeting of Constantine and Licinius at Milan, showing the heads of Constantine and the Sun side by side.

During the years that he authorised these pagan issues, Constantine can hardly have been in the full sense of the word a Christian. He was undoubtedly a patron and a devotee of the highest divinity whom the Christians worshipped; but he does not yet seem to have realised that this divinity was a jealous God who tolerated no partners or even subordinates. The story of Constantine's conversion perhaps helps to explain his religious position in the years which followed.

Eusebius in his *Life of Constantine,* which he wrote soon after the Emperor's death in 337, is the first to record the heavenly vision of the Cross. He himself knew nothing of it when he wrote the ninth book of his *Church History* soon after the fall of Maxentius and Maximin. Lactantius, when he wrote his treatise *On the Deaths of the Persecutors* during the same period, knew nothing of it; according to him, it was in a dream on the night before the battle of the Milvian Bridge that Constantine was instructed to mark "the heavenly sign of God" on the shields of the soldiers. This statement of Lactantius is evidence that Constantine's troops did bear the sacred monogram on their shields at the battle of the Milvian Bridge, but the dream may be no more historial than the angel who dictated to Licinius his monotheistic prayer.

But if they story of the heavenly vision is slow to make its appearance, it rests on the best of authority. For Eusebius informs us that "the victorious Emperor himself told the story to me, the author of this work, many years afterwards, when I was esteemed worthy of his acquaintance and familiarity, and confirmed it upon oath." . . .

There is no reason to doubt the *bona fides* of either Eusebius or Constantine. The vagueness of the setting in which the incident is placed bears the stamp of truth. If the vision were a fiction it would surely have been placed at some dramatic moment, like Lactantius' dream, not when Constantine was marching "somewhere" unspecified. It is indeed curious that there is no contemporary record of the heavenly vision, but it may well have been less conspicuous than Constantine imagined it later to have been. It is, moreover, evident from the way in which Eusebius introduces the story that Constantine had never given any publicity to his experience: it was only when they had got on to terms of intimacy that the Emperor revealed to him his proud secret.

What Constantine probably saw was a rare, but well-attested, form of the "halo phenomenon." This is a phenomenon analogous to the rainbow, and like it local and transient, caused by the fall, not of rain, but of ice crystals across the rays of the sun. It usually takes the form of mock suns or of rings of light surrounding the sun, but a cross of light with the sun in its centre has been on several occasions scientifically observed. The display may well have been brief and unspectacular, but to Constantine's overwrought imagination it was deeply significant. It was to the Sun that he now especially paid his devotion, and in his hour of need the Sun had sent him a sign; and that sign was the Cross, the symbol of the Christians. Whatever this signified, that Christ was a manifestation of the Unconquered Sun, or that the Sun was the symbol of the Heavenly Power whom the Christians worshipped, it was manifest that Christ, the Lord of the Cross, was to be his champion and protector.

It was not the Cross which Constantine used as the emblem of his new patron god, but a monogram, ☧, composed of the first two Greek letters of the word Christos, Chi and Rho. It was this sign that he painted on the shields of his soldiers before the final battle, and that he himself henceforth wore on his helmet: it was, moreover, the distinctive feature of the Labarum. From the careful description which Lactantius gives of its form, it is evident that the monogram was something new to him and his Latin public,

and though it was commonly employed in Greek as an abbreviation for other words beginning with Chi and Rho, it appears never to have been used before Constantine's day as a Christian symbol. It must have been Constantine's own idea to make the abbreviation into a heraldic emblem of his divine champion.

Confident in the support of the Christian God, Constantine put his powers to a severe test. The Gallic orator who in the summer of 313 congratulated the Emperor on his victory of the previous autumn, no doubt exaggerated the risks which he had run in order to magnify the glory of his final victory. But there was a considerable degree of truth in his remarks. Maxentius had very large forces at his disposal, and had taken great pains to ingratiate himself with his troops by lavish generosity. Not only Severus but the great Galerius himself, had failed dismally in their efforts to unseat him. Yet Constantine embarked on his attack single-handed, and employed for it only a quarter of his troops. Such confidence is hardly explicable, had not Constantine felt himself assured of Divine favour.

His spectacular victory naturally confirmed Constantine's faith in the Christian God, and he resolved to take appropriate measures to express his gratitude and to win further favour. He had apparently, even before his victory, attached to himself as his religious adviser a Spanish bishop, Hosius of Corduba, and he took his expert advice, as we have seen, in distributing benefactions to the Church. But there is no evidence that he sought or received instruction in the faith. He had not been converted by any human missionary, but by a heavenly sign from God Himself, and he seems for the time being to have formed his own ideas on the appropriate way to win God's favour. This was in his view to grant liberty, subsidies and immunities to the body of initiates who conducted the cult of the Supreme Divinity, the Church. Soon he was to learn that discord in His Church was hateful to the Divinity, and that in order to maintain His favour he must preserve its unity and harmony. But he does not yet appear to have realised that he would offend the Supreme Divinity by paying respect to other gods, and in particular to the Unconquered Sun, whom he in some sort identified with the Christian God. Did not the Christians themselves meet for prayer on the day of the sun, and in their prayers turn towards the rising sun? And was it not written in their holy books that God was the Sun of Righteousness?

It may seem strange that the bishops, whom he met with increasing frequency, did not sooner enlighten him on this point. But they were probably only too thankful to secure toleration and favour after the horrors of persecution. Constantine, like Maximin, might change his mind: it was safer not to provoke the Emperor and meanwhile to receive the subsidies and immunities which he showered upon the Church. It would be a bold man who offered unsolicited advice to a Roman emperor, and none of the bishops seems to have felt called upon to instruct Constantine, much less to rebuke him for his errors.

Constantine's legislation during the next decade bears out this analysis of his religious position. On the one hand he extended additional privileges to the Church. In 318 he ordained that a civil suit might, with the consent of both parties, be removed to the jurisdiction of a bishop, even when it had already begun in an imperial court, and that the bishop's verdict should be final. In 321 he legalised bequests to the Church, and enacted that manumissions performed in church before the bishop should have full legal

validity, the slaves so freed becoming Roman citizens, and furthermore that the clergy might free their own slaves by will with full legal effect. It was also probably during this period that Constantine built the Basilica Constantiniana in the Lateran, with its Baptistery, the Fons Constantini, and endowed them with lands bringing in an annual revenue of 4,390 and 10,234 solidi respectively. For the lands which were bestowed on these churches all lay in the West, mainly in Italy, Sicily and Africa, with small quantities in Gaul and Greece (which he acquired in 314), whereas other Roman churches, endowed later, were given eastern lands. Other laws show traces of Christian influence. In 316 he prohibited the branding of convicts on the face, "that the face, which is formed in the likeness of the heavenly beauty, may not be disfigured," and in 320 he repealed the disabilities which Augustus had imposed on celibates, male and female, and on married persons who were childless.

His legislation on Sunday observance is a more doubtful case. In March 321, he enacted that on "the venerable day of the Sun" the law courts and all workshops should be closed and the urban population should rest: the rural population were, however, commanded to continue their labours, lest by missing the right moment the crops provided by the Heavenly Providence should perish. A second law, issued a few months later, confirms that "the day celebrated by the veneration of the Sun" ought not to be occupied with contentious legal proceedings, but permits manumissions and emancipations on Sundays. The idea of Sunday as a day of rest is Christian, but it is noteworthy that Constantine does not call it, according to the current Christian practice, the Lord's Day, but on the contrary emphasises its sacredness to the Sun. It would appear that Constantine imagined that Christian observance of the first day of the planetary week was a tribute to the Unconquered Sun.

Various laws dealing with magic and divination also reveal the ambiguity of Constantine's position. The private practice of both had long been illegal, and Constantine was making no innovation in prohibiting them. Towards magic he is, in a law dated 318, unusually mild, for while he subjects to severe penalties those who employ magic arts against the lives or the chastity of their neighbours, he expressly permits spells for the cure of illness or for preventing rain or hail storms from spoiling the vintage. He deals with divination in three laws issued in 319 and 320. In two of them he prohibits soothsayers from entering private houses, even on the pretext of personal friendship with the owner; the penalty is for the soothsayer to be burned alive and for his host to be deported to an island after confiscation of his property. In both laws persons wishing to foretell the future are expressly authorised to do so publicly in the temples — "You who think it to your interest, go to the public altars and temples and celebrate the rites of your traditional faith; for we do not prohibit the ceremonies of past practice to be performed in the light of day." The third law shows that Constantine did not, at this date, see any harm in consulting soothsayers himself on appropriate occasions. It runs: "If it be established that any part of our palace or of other public buildings has been struck by lightning, the practice currently observed should be maintained and the soothsayers be asked what it portends, and their reports having been carefully collected should be referred to our notice. Leave is also to be given to others for observing

this custom, provided that they refrain from domestic sacrifices, which are specifically prohibited."

It has often been remarked that Constantine felt no scruple at retaining the title of Pontifex Maximus. This point is not very significant, since not only did Constantine himself continue to hold it in his later years, when he was undoubtedly a Christian, but later Christian emperors down to Gratian did the same. The title was a traditional appanage of the office of Augustus, and involved no participation in pagan rites. It merely gave its holder rights of supervision and control over religion, and was as such as useful to a Christian as to a pagan emperor. Nor is it significant that Constantine, in 312, authorised the creation of a new provincial priesthood of Africa in honour of his family, the *gens Flavia. . . .*

Constantine's conversion may be said to have been in a sense a religious experience, since, though his dominating motive was the achievement of worldly power, he relied for that end, not on human but on divine aid. But it was not a spiritual experience. Constantine knew and cared nothing for the metaphysical and ethical teaching of Christianity when he became a devotee of the Christian God: he simply wished to enlist on his side a powerful divinity, Who had, he believed, spontaneously offered him a sign. His conversion was initially due to a meteorological phenomenon which he happened to witness at a critical moment of his career. But this fortuitous event ultimately led to Constantine's genuinely adopting the Christian Faith, to the conversion of the Roman Empire, and to the Christian civilisation of Europe.

With the publication of his *Constantin der Grosse* in 1949 JOSEPH VOGT (b.1895), professor of ancient history at Tübingen, became one of the important contributors to Constantinian studies. In the following selection from his more recent survey of the late empire, Vogt attempts to construct from the disparate fragments of information a composite picture of Constantine's religious attitudes and policies.*

**Joseph Vogt**

# *The Universal Monarchy*

Today the age of Constantine is linked in people's minds with the epoch-making action of the emperor in granting to the Church, after its period of persecution, not merely recognition but also partnership with the state, so that it was placed in a position of wealth and power. It is pointed out that two dangerous courses were now open to the Church: it might entertain political ambitions and seek to subdue states, emperors and princes—a line of ecclesiastical policy followed in western Europe during the Middle Ages; or it might submit to the orders of the ruler and become an instrument of state— the risk run by the Byzantine church. Some of those who take this long-distance view are impatient of the role still played by state-churches in many countries, wishing to see the last of the new era ushered in by Constantine; the Church, it is said, should shed all political power and concentrate on the salvation of men's souls, if need be at the price of returning to the catacombs. Leaving the problems of the contemporary world to one side, if we concentrate on the fate of antiquity it is obvious that Constantine was indeed responsible for historic decisions which deeply influenced the later course of ancient civilization. In his long reign he destroyed the tetrarchy and its pagan theology but at the same time, by refashioning the system of absolute government, did even more than his predecessors to stabilize the framework of the Roman

*From Joseph Vogt, *The Decline of Rome*, translated by J. Sondheimer (London: George Weidenfeld & Nicholson, Ltd., 1965), pp. 87–95. Reprinted by permission of George Weidenfeld & Nicholson, Ltd., and the New American Library. Footnotes omitted.

empire. Leading state and Church in dou-
ble harness, he was the first emperor to
take a lead in church affairs and the first
to entrust the Church with public respon-
sibilities. There can be no doubt that this
was a momentous revolution, and to demonstrate that this was so we shall have to
concentrate on the emperor's actions, on
the factual record of his reign. Only passing allusion can be made to the much-
debated subject of his character, which
turns on the question whether his policy
towards the Church was determined sole-
ly by his thirst for power and by reasons
of state or in part also by sincere devotion to the new faith. The various authorities give very different accounts of the
matter. While pagan chroniclers leave
a great deal to conjecture, Christians
interpret the emperor's actions wholly
in their favour. Lactantius, in his *De
mortibus persecutorum* which covers
events down to the year in which it appeared (about 318), waxes quite fanatical
in his efforts to prove that all persecutors
came to a horrible end, contrasting their
fate with the blessings bestowed on Constantine and Licinius, guardians of the
faith. Eusebius, bishop of Caesarea in
Palestine and from 325 a personal friend
of Constantine, in his *Ecclesiastical History* and still more in his *Life of Constantine,* sets out to portray the emperor as the
man of Providence who through his deeds
enabled the divine Logos to penetrate the
world. Fortunately many of Constantine's
own letters, edicts and laws have survived,
together with inscriptions, coins, buildings and portraits, and it is these self-
revelations which must form the basis of
our historical interpretation of his epoch.

This much is clear: Constantine, son of
Constantius and Helena, deviated from
the path marked out by the tetrarchy and
from its religious basis right from the
start. When Diocletian re-formed the te-

trarchy in 305 Constantine and Maxentius
(the son of Maximian) were passed over:
in the following year both were acclaimed
Caesars by their own armies, amongst
whom dynastic sentiment was still strong.
Constantine and Maxentius now stood in
opposition to the legitimate rulers Galerius, Maximinus Daia, Severus and Licinius. This cleavage shows itself in their
religious policies. While the rulers of the
east kept up an almost uninterrupted
persecution of the Christians, Maxentius,
the effective ruler of Italy and Africa,
was conciliatory, while remaining staunch
in his personal allegiance to the old gods.
As ruler of Gaul and Britain, Constantine
continued the tolerating policy of his father; father and son were apparently alike
in dissociating themselves from popular
polytheism. Portrait coins issued in 310
show that Constantine had accepted the
sun-god as his personal protector. In the
same year a panegyrist declares that Constantine is Caesar by right of birth, and
through the grace of the sun-god may
expect to receive a universal empire. The
assertion that Constantine was called to a
single rule by the highest god is clear in-
dication that he was setting himself up
against the tetrarchical system and its
representatives in the east—the language
of the coins and the panegyric must have
been inspired by Constantine himself. But
however bold the hopes he entertained
for the future, Constantine was skilful
enough to concentrate his immediate efforts towards an objective which the death
of Galerius appeared to bring within his
reach: the overthrow of Maxentius, which
would give him control of the central
regions of the empire. In the eyes of the
rulers of the east Maxentius had always
been and continued to be a usurper; in
Italy and Rome his oppressive political
measures had lost him support among the
population. In 312 therefore Constantine

embarked on a war which he claimed as a war of liberation, to free the people from the yoke of tyranny. A conquering progress over the Alps and the Appennines was crowned on 28 October by the victory at the Milvian Bridge, a league north of Rome, which cost Maxentius both his rule and his life. After a triumphal entry into Rome Constantine was recognized by the senate as Augustus of the first rank.

In Christian tradition the battle at the Milvian Bridge is linked with Constantine's personal decision to turn to the God of the Christians. When all the evidence is weighed it becomes quite clear that from this time onward Constantine recognized in the God of the Christians a giver of victory; and whether or not one describes this recognition as conversion, it certainly prompted Constantine to some far-reaching conclusions. Lactantius relates that in the night before the decisive battle Constantine was advised in a dream to mark the shields of his soldiers with the heavenly sign of God, and that he carried out his instructions by ordering a sign of Christ to be placed on the shields; from Lactantius' description the sign appears to have been the monogrammatic cross ☧. On the other hand, Eusebius in his *Ecclesiastical History* says merely that Constantine invoked Christ as his ally in the war. In his life of the emperor, however, Eusebius mentions that Constantine experienced a vision at the outset of the campaign in which he saw a cross of light standing over the sun, accompanied by the words "In this sign conquer"; this manifestation was followed by a nocturnal vision in which Constantine was guided to use the sign to protect himself against the enemy, whereupon he had a standard prepared bearing a sign in which the letters X and P crossed to produce the contracted name of Christ, the Chi-Rho monogram ☧. However much these accounts differ in detail, they show remarkable agreement in insisting that the sign Constantine actually used was not the plain cross of his vision but a cross which he transformed into a monogram identifying Christ as the victory-giving God. In the manifestos he issued in the years which followed, Constantine repeatedly pays tribute to this God who in times of persecution endowed his worshippers with the strength to endure martyrdom and to overcome. It is plain that Constantine was assisted to his appreciation of the Christian religion by his need for a divine ally in combat. If this God was really capable of such victories, then—in keeping with the traditional Roman view—it should also be possible to win his support through the appropriate ritual acts, for example invoking the power of his name. It was also imperative to see that this protective deity continued to bestow his favours on the state. An experience of this kind, and the gloss Constantine put upon it, was certainly no conversion in the New Testament sense; it more closely resembles the assimilation of a new god after the old Roman fashion.

It is essential to bear in mind that Constantine did not suppress all other deities after the victory at the Milvian Bridge. He was even careful to see that the God of the Christians was not mentioned by name in the few official documents referring to the victory. A panegyric of 313 mentions that Constantine received a special revelation from on high, but goes into no details. The old gods long retained their place on the coinage, whereas Christian symbols were only gradually adopted, and it was some years before their meaning became standardized. In 315 the Roman senate dedicated the triumphal arch erected at the Flavian amphitheatre in honour of Constantine's victory. A frieze running right round it chronicles in traditional style the whole course of the war, from the time the emperor moved camp to the concluding acts of state, taking in the conquest of Verona, the battle at the bridge and entry into Rome. In the portions where the emperor is shown addressing the people and distributing his gratuity, he stares out at the beholder from the centre of the picture, present in all his majesty—the same hieratical stance we have observed in historical reliefs of the preceding period. But there is no reference to the new tutelary deity; here the victory-giving figure is the sun-god. It must be remembered that the arch expressed the views of the Roman senate, which was still wholly loyal to paganism. The inscription merely makes a cryptic reference to the victory obtained "through divine inspiration" *(instinctu divinitatis)*.

But we have other witnesses to the piety of the new ruler of Rome and from these we learn that Constantine gave public expression to his gratitude to his divine patron. The magnificent silver medallion, whose obverse and reverse depicts the conquest and liberation of the city, was probably struck at the mint of Ticinum (near Milan) as early as 313; and on the obverse the monogram appears, on the crested plume of Constantine's helmet. In a prestige issue of this type, the incorporation of the Christ-monogram into the portrait of the emperor could only have been done on the highest authority. Perhaps the most conclusive manifestation of Constantine's acceptance of the new faith was the transformation of the most majestic of all Roman buildings, which was carried out between 313 and 315. The enormous three-aisled basilica erected by Maxentius on the eastern edge of the Forum Romanum was now dedicated by the senate to Constantine, his conqueror. The apse of the basilica, where the judges should have held court, was filled with a statue of the world-ruler, seven times life-size. The colossal head now stands in the court of the Conservatori Palace at Rome: a truly imperial portrait in which the features of the individual are almost wholly obliterated beneath the dignity of the supreme world-ruler, in the words of a court poet *sanctus Caesar, omnipotens Augustus*. Eusebius probably has this statue in mind when he relates (in the *Ecclesiastical History*) how Constantine ordered that an enormous statue erected to him at Rome by the Senate should show him with the saving sign of victory—the Christ-monogram—in his hand.

For Constantine the statesman, display of the victory sign was of secondary importance compared with the need to secure the lasting benevolence of the new God towards the state. This accounts for his prompt action in making over the palace of the Laterani to the bishop of Rome (in the winter of 312–3) and in sponsoring a number of monumental churches within the city. This action becomes all the more significant when we remember that although the Christians had had their burial ground (the catacombs) in the old capital, as yet they had no church there. Hitherto their meetings had been held in private houses adapted for liturgical purposes. The church now built at the Lateran was a five-aisled basilica modelled on secular buildings of this type; it was followed a little later by the basilica in honour of Saints Marcellinus and Peter, martyred under Diocletian. Constantine thus acknowledged that at Rome itself the state was under an obligation to support the Christian religion. He also did everything possible to secure recognition for the new status of Christianity throughout the empire. In the east Maximinus Daia had flouted the Galerian edict of toleration and was again persecuting Christians. But in February 313, at a meeting in Milan,

Constantine persuaded Licinius, ruler of the Danubian and Balkan provinces, to join with him in making Christianity a protected religion everywhere in the empire. Admittedly, no edict issued from this conference, but the programme decided upon can be gathered from rescripts sent by Licinius to the governors of the eastern provinces, after his defeat of Maximinus Daia had brought the whole East under his control. From these it appears that the emperors had decided "to give to Christians as to all others free choice to follow the religion they desired, so that whatever exists of Divinity and Celestial Reality may be amicable and propitious towards us and our subjects." Joined to this general declaration was an explicit statement that the Christian persecution was at an end, that the communities were to have their confiscated properties and meeting-places freely restored to them. The programme initiated at Milan thus goes much further than the toleration edict of Galerius: the new faith is acknowledged as the source of victory, the Christian communities are recognized in due form as corporations capable of possessing legal rights, their existence as organized entities is endorsed.

During the years which followed the parts of the empire ruled by Constantine were left in no doubt that he was determined to accept the full consequences of making Christianity part of the state religion. A schism had arisen in Africa over the question of whether and in what form Christians whose faith had weakened under the Diocletian persecution could be readmitted to fellowship. Caecilian, who had been elected bishop of Carthage in 312, was rejected by many other bishops of the region on the grounds that he had been consecrated by a bishop who had surrendered the scriptures when required to do so by the state inquisitors. The pur-

ists declared the consecration invalid and elected an anti-bishop, Maiorinus, who was to be succeeded in 315 by Donatus, the powerful leader from whom the schism takes its name. Other African cities soon had their Donatist communities, founded in opposition to the churches led by Caecilian; and the Donatists even went to the length of rebaptising Christians who came over to them from the old Church. Some scholars have thought that in seceding from the main, the Catholic Church, the Donatists were directly inspired by the concept of the Church held by Cyprian, the martyr-bishop of Carthage, and that they made this theological position the basis of their claim to autonomy. Any such hypothesis is quite implausible; what is possible, however, is that in Donatist radicalism a fundamentally semitic vein in African Christianity was working itself to the surface. It can be shown that the Donatist church attracted strongest support in Numidia, among the section of the population still imprinted by Berber and Punic influences, that is to say among peoples still incompletely romanized. In these regions, moreover, Donatism found most of its adherents among the lower classes, whose rejection of the Church of Carthage can also be interpreted as an act of hostility towards Roman officials and still more towards Roman proprietors. These sentiments account for the attraction the Donatist church held for the revolutionary movement of the Circumcellions, a terrorist rising of peasant fanatics with a very varied following, which was soon to break out.

The threat of agrarian unrest had yet to declare itself when Constantine first intervened in African affairs. If we accept his own oft-repeated explanation of his actions in Africa, it seems that his primary aim was to ensure that African Christians were worshipping God in due form, so as to protect the welfare of the state. This again sheds light on Constantine's personal attitude towards the new religion. Had he still, in the spirit of a Diocletian, regarded observance of the Roman state religion as the prerequisite for securing divine favour, he could only have welcomed the schism among the Christians. As it was, he believed his duty to the common good obliged him to maintain unity within the Christian faith, and he accordingly went into action, without a full appreciation of what he was doing. A letter to the governor of Africa ordering the restoration of confiscated Christian property was followed by a second which exempted priests of the Catholic Church from all municipal obligations—a tacit avowal that the clerical order, as a professional body, performed work essential to the state. On this occasion, as later, we find that the church of Caecilian is described as the Catholic Church, a designation which earlier writers had employed to describe a Church universal, comprehending the whole empire. There can be little doubt that this line in ecclesiastical thinking had the support of bishop Hosius, now coming to the fore as the emperor's adviser on Christian affairs. In a letter to Caecilian, the emperor speaks of "the lawful and most holy Christian religion," castigating the schismatics as men of insubordinate temper and hinting that the services of state officials could be called on to enforce their return to the fold. But the Donatists also placed their trust in the emperor and petitioned him to appoint unbiased judges from Gaul to settle the dispute. Constantine agreed to appoint judges but directed Miltiades, bishop of Rome, to investigate and decide the affair. The tribunal Miltiades set up, in effect a Roman synod, passed sentence of excommunication on Donatus. The Donatists appealed from this judgement

to the emperor, who took the momentous step of summoning a synod composed of bishops from all the lands under his rule, to meet in August 314, at Arles, in Gaul.

This marks the first occasion on which an episcopal synod was used as a tool of imperial policy. The council of Arles confirmed the condemnation of Donatus and in recognition of the emperor's good offices passed resolutions whose effect was to bring Christians into closer partnership with Constantine's state: Christians were expressly given permission to hold offices which entailed frequent attendance at feasts and games, while avoidance of military service by Christians now incurred the threat of ecclesiastical penalties. The emperor was thus assured that loyal Catholic subjects could be won by means of a synod. But the Donatists were still dissatisfied and appealed to the tribunal of the emperor himself. Constantine's first reaction was to try to persuade the two leaders of the warring churches to leave Africa; when this failed, he resorted to threats and declared in writing his intention of coming in person to deliver judgement. For, he said, it was his duty "to exterminate errors and staunch all follies, and so see to it that all men profess the true religion in open harmony, offering Almighty God due worship." Here once again we have a clear statement of a concept basic to Roman rule, that the safety of the state rests on the true worship of divinity. Even this threat failed, however, and unrest in Africa mounted. At length officials were forced to intervene and Donatists were prosecuted; now that they were the persecuted element in an empire in process of becoming Christian, the Donatists could claim that their communities were the true martyr-churches. In 321, after many bitter experiences, Constantine granted the Donatist Church a limited measure of toleration. It was after this, with the fully conscious intention of defending what was the business of the Church from intervention by the state, that Donatus greeted an imperial embassy with the question "What has the emperor to do with the Church?" while his adherents accused the Catholic Church of betraying the Christians' Lord in order to win Caesar's favour.

Such was the upshot of the first encounter between a Christian emperor and the Christian Church. We have seen the emperor trying to make the Christian religion serve the state, just as the Roman religion had done in the past. While the Church of the mainstream was prepared to meet him, the Donatist Church, despite appeals made by its spokesmen direct to the emperor, now turned away from the state and persisted as a protest movement, at once religious and social. Just how far the Catholic Church, in its new situation, was breaking out of its restricted circle and invading public life is shown by many of the decisions and constitutions belonging to this period. Constantine made bishops privileged dignitaries and entrusted them with official duties. A law of 316 legalized the enfranchisement of slaves in church in the presence of the bishop as a new form of manumission. This was followed two years later by official recognition of the bishop's jurisdiction, which had long been acknowledged in practice within the Christian communities, as authoritative in civil cases. Next, individual churches secured the right of receiving legacies under wills, which not only confirmed their existence as legal personalities but also made it easier to build up their resources. In 321 Sunday was declared a public holiday, which marked the acceptance of the Christian Lord's Day by the state. These singular concessions raised the Catholic Church above all other religions and communities. Yet

Constantine still continued as the High Priest of the Roman state *(pontifex maximus)* and as such remained responsible for the worship of the gods, even though he himself no longer took part in pagan ceremonies. As under his predecessors, certain pagan practices might be forbidden for the sake of public order (secret soothsaying, for example); but paganism retained its official position. Pagans were still being appointed to key offices in the administration and the army and the first duty of the emperor, even a Christian emperor, was still to defend the frontiers of the empire and secure the well-being of all its subjects.

Constantine and Licinius (who after his victory over Maximinus Daia in 313 ruled the eastern part of the empire), were frequently at variance; but it seems that the peace they concluded in 317 was a genuine effort at co-existence. Licinius was in any case engaged in strenuous efforts to raise the level of economic life in the eastern provinces. In his policy towards the Christians he adhered to the toleration agreed on at Milan, without incorporating the organization of the Church—much stronger here than in the provinces governed by Constantine—into that of the state. The more firmly Constantine bound his bishops to the state, the more emphatic became Licinius in asserting his independence of the Church; indeed from 320 he started to favour pagans in his administration and army at the expense of Christians and went so far as to forbid episcopal synods, suppressing all overt Christian opposition by force. In view of these and other differences, one might describe the relationship between the two rulers as a cold war. At length both sides began preparations for an open conflict. The issue at stake was whether Constantine could realize what had always been his aim, a universal monarchy; but the stuggle also turned into a war of religion, since Constantine went into battle under the victory-standard of Christ, while Licinius took care to solicit the favour of the old gods through elaborate sacrifices. In the autumn of 324, after bitter fighting on land and sea, Licinius was defeated at Chrysopolis, on Asian soil; soon afterwards, because of his attempt at allying with the Danubian peoples, Licinius was executed as an enemy of the state. Constantine, the champion of Christianity, had made himself sole ruler of the empire.

# Suggestions for Further Reading

Included in this brief and necessarily selective bibliography are books and articles which (1) provide a general survey of third- and fourth-century political and religious developments, (2) assess the ancient evidence of Constantine's religious attitudes and policies, and (3) support one of the three modern interpretations of the conversion. Although studies which appeared before 1929 (the year in which Norman H. Baynes published his Raleigh Lecture) generally have been omitted, it should not be inferred that these are unimportant. On the contrary, most of the ideas and theories discussed by recent scholars were proposed before that date. Those who wish to read the earlier literature should consult the magisterial appendix to Bayne's lecture. The most recent and comprehensive of the general bibliographical guides are the two essays by J. Vogt, "Constantinus der Grosse," *Reallexikon für Antike und Christentum,* 3 (Stuttgart, 1956), 306–379 and "Bemerkungen zum Gang der Constantinforschung "in *Mullus: Festschrift T. Klauser* (Münster, 1964), pp. 374–379. Annual additions to the bibliography are listed in J. Marouzeau et al., *L'Année philologique* (Paris, 1928–     ).

Two outstanding examples of the increasing interest in the third and fourth centuries are the complementary, but conceptually dissimilar syntheses of A. H. M. Jones, *The Later Roman Empire, 284–602* (London, 1964)—see also his less detailed distillation, *The Decline of the Ancient World* (New York, 1966)—and J. Vogt, *The Decline of Rome,* translated by J. Sondheimer (London, 1965). An older, but durable assessment is E. Stein, *Histoire du Bas–Empire,* vol. 1 (Paris, 1959), translated and equipped with excellent, up-to-date notes by J.-R. Palanque. The most stimulating of the one-volume surveys of the fourth century is A. Piganiol, *L'Empire Chrétien* (Paris, 1947), which traces political and ideological developments from the later years of Constantine's reign (325) to the death of Theodosius I (395).

To appreciate the significance of Constantine's break with the legacy of pagan-Christian hostility, some knowledge of Church history, Church-State conflicts, and contemporary ideological warfare is essential. The most informative of the general histories of the Christian Church is A. Fliche and V. Martin (eds.) *Histoire de l'église* (Paris, 1934–     ). The fourth century is treated in volume 3, *De la Paix Constantinienne à la mort de Théodose* by P. de Labriolle, G. Bardy, and J.-R. Palanque (Paris, 1947), published in English as *The Church in the Christian Roman Empire* (London, 1949). Another in this genre, but with a rather different approach to Church history, is H. Lietzmann, *A History of the Early Church,* translated by B. L. Wolff (London, 1961); volume 3 covers the period from Constantine to Julian. Among the many books that analyze religious developments during Constantine's reign, the following are representative and instructive: H. von Schoenebeck, *Beiträge zur Religionspolitik des Maxentius und Constantin,* Klio Beiheft 43, N. S. Heft 30 (1939); H. Doerries, *Das Selbstzeugnis Kaiser Konstantins* (Göttingen, 1954); H. Kraft, *Kaiser Konstantins Religiöse Entwicklung* (Tübingen, 1955); S. Calderone, *Constantino e il Cattolicesimo,* I (Florence, 1962), especially part ii, and most recently Ramsay MacMullen, *Constantine* (New York, 1969). All of these assess Constantine's religious policies, and two (Kraft, Doerries) provide a useful compendium of the relevant ancient documents. They should be read, therefore, in conjunction with the interpretations of the conversion listed below.

A thoughtful and very readable introduction to the history of official persecution from the first century to the "Great Persecution" of the fourth is J. Moreau, *La Persécution du Christianisme dans l'empire romain* (Paris, 1956), chap. 6. The fundamental analysis (with up-to-date notes, bibliography, and excurses on a variety of special topics) is H. Grégoire, J. Moreau et al., *Les Persécutions dans l'empire romain* (Memoires, Académie Royale de Belgique, Classe des Lettres 2, lvi, v, 1964). Also useful are the bibliographical essays of J. Vogt, "Christenverfolgung, I (Historisch)," *Reallexikon für Antike und Christentum,* 2 (Stuttgart, 1954), pp. 1159–1208, and H. Last, "Christenverfolgung II (juristisch)," *idem,* pp. 1208–1228. The general historical background is examined in three recent books: A. D. Momigliano (ed.), *The Conflict between Paganism and Christianity in the Fourth Century* (London, 1963); E. R. Dodds, *Pagan and Christian in an Age of Anxiety* (London, 1965); W. H. C. Frend, *Martyrdom and Persecution in the Early Christian Church* (London, 1965), with a discussion of the "Great Persecution" in chapter 15, pp. 477–535. Constitutional questions arising from the conflict are analyzed by H. U. Instinsky, *Bischofstuhle und Kaiserthron* (Munich, 1955); J. Gaudemet, *L'Église dans l'empire romain IVe–Ve Siécles* (Histoire du droit et des institutions de l'église en Occident III, Paris, 1958); and K. F. Morrison, *Rome and the City of God* (Transactions American Philosophical Society n.s. 54, pt. 1, 1964).

As the Tetrarchs created a new and rather exclusive set of symbols to express the eternality of the Roman state—for example, the association of the Augusti and Caesars with either Hercules or Jupiter—it is not surprising that the Church-State conflict was increasingly imbued with a kind of ideological gamesmanship. For a commentary on Christian attitudes in this struggle for symbolic supremacy, see K. Setton, *Christian Attitudes towards the Emperor in the Fourth Century* (New York, 1941); cf. F. Dvornik, *Early Christian and Byzantine Political Philosophy* (Dumbarton Oaks, Washington, 1966), a general introduction to politi-

cal theory in the third and fourth centuries. Attempts to reinforce the emperor's divine association through art and monumental architecture, and thus to illustrate his special and unassailable role in the administration of the divine cosmos, are traced in two excellent books by H. P. L'Orange: *Studies on the Iconography of Cosmic Kingship in the Ancient World* (Institut for Sammenlignende Kulturforskning, A, 23, Oslo, 1953) and *Art Forms and Civic Life in the Late Roman Empire* (Princeton, N.J., 1965).

The first literary account of the events of October 312 is contained in the book nine of Eusebius, *Ecclesiastical History,* probably completed in 315. A number of general introductions to the life and work of this remarkable scholar and ecclesiastical politician have been published in recent years: D. S. Wallace-Hadrill, *Eusebius of Caesarea* (London, 1960); J. Quasten, *Patrology,* III (Utrecht, 1960), pp. 309–345; J. Moreau, "Eusebius von Caesarea," *Reallexikon für Antike und Christentum,* 6 (Stuttgart, 1965), pp. 1052–1088, which includes a bibliography down to 1961. English translations of the *Ecclesiastical History* are available in the Loeb Classical Library (with Greek text), by K. Lake and J. E. L. Oulton (London, 1926–1932), and in a Penguin Classics paperback, by G. Williamson (New York, 1966).

The fundamental treatment of Lactantius' pamphlet *On the Deaths of the Persecutors*—considered by many the most trustworthy of the three literary accounts—is J. Moreau, *Lactance, De la Mort des Persécuteurs* (Paris, 1954); edition with French translation in volume 1, an exhaustive commentary in volume 2. An English translation by W. Fletcher is available in volume 22 of the *Ante-Nicene Christian Library* (Edinburgh, 1871). Moreau's conclusion that Lactantius wrote the treatise between 318 and 320 has not satisfied everyone: J. Stevenson, "The Life and Literacy Activity of Lactantius," *Studia Patristica,* I, Texte und Untersuchungen zur Geschichte der Altchristlichen Literatur, 63 (Berlin, 1957), pp. 661–677, prefers 317; J.-R. Palanque, "Sur la Date du De Mortibus Persecutorum," *Mélanges offerts à J. Carcopino* (Paris, 1966), pp. 711–716 assigns the work to the years 313–315.

The most complex, and in many ways the most important, source problem is presented by the *Life of Constantine*, which has been the central focus of the debate over Constantine's conversion. The classic critique of the *Life* is H. Grégoire's article "Eusèbe n'est pas l'auteur de la 'vita Constantini' dans sa forme actuelle et Constantin ne s'est pas 'converti' en 312," *Byzantion*, 13 (1938), 561–583; cf. also "L'Authenticité et l'historicité de la 'vita Constantini' attribuée à Eusèbe de Césarée," *Bulletin de la Classe des lettres et des sciences morales et politiques*, 39 (1953), 462–478; G. Downey, "The Builder of the Original Church of the Apostles at Constantinople," *Dumbarton Oaks Papers*, 6 (1951), 53–80 (especially pp. 57–66, where he puts forward the view that the *Life*, as we have it, was "revised" after Eusebius' death); P. Orgels, "A propos des erreurs historiques de la 'vita Constantini' attribuée à Eusèbe," *Annuaire de l'Institut de Philologie et d'histoire Orientales et Slaves*, 21 (1953), 575–611. The Eusebian authorship of the *Life* and the authenticity of the documents contained in it have been defended by I. Daniele, *I Documenti Constantiniensi della 'Vita Constantini' di Eusebio de Cesarea*, in *Analecta Gregoriana*, 13 (Ser. Fac. Hist. Eccles., Sect. BI, Rome, 1938); F. Franchi di' Cavalieri, *Constantiniana* (Studi e Testi 171, Vatican City, 1953), pp. 67–179; A. H. M. Jones and T. C. Skeat, "Notes on the Genuineness of the Constantinian Documents in Eusebius' Life of Constantine," *Journal of Ecclesiastical History*, 5 (1954), 196–200; W. Telfer, "The Author's Purpose in the Vita Constantini," *Studia Patristica*, I, Texte und Untersuchungen zur Geschichte der Altchristlichen Literatur, 63 (Berlin, 1957), pp. 157–167; and F. Winkelmann, the most active participant in the debate recently, in "Zur Geschichte des Authentizstäts problems der Vita Constantini," *Klio*, 40 (1962), 187–243. The main outlines of the problem have now been delineated by scholars; each reader of the *Life* must assess the issues and decide the question of reliability for himself.

One other literary source deserves mention —the pagan panegyrics of 310, 311, 313 and 321, all of which are dedicated to Constantine: Latin text edited by R. A. B. Mynors (London, 1964), text and French translation by E. Galletier (Paris, 1949). As we have seen, certain passages from these "official" publications have been cited as proof of Constantine's syncretic intentions.

Integration of the extensive numismatic evidence from Constantine's reign has been greatly facilitated in recent years by the publications of M. R. Alföldi, *Die Constantinische Goldprägung* (Mainz, 1963) and P. Bruun, *Roman Imperial Coinage, VII. Constantine and Licinius, A.D. 313–337* (London, 1966). The pioneer in this field was Andreas Alföldi, who put forward the view that the Christian monogram is depicted on the helmet of Constantine which appears on medallions struck at Ticinum around 315: see his articles "The Helmet of Constantine with the Christian Monogram," *Journal of Roman Studies*, 22 (1932), 9–23, and "The Initials of Christ on the Helmet of Constantine," *Studies in Roman Economic and Social History in Honor of A. C. Johnson* (Princeton, N.J., 1951), pp. 303–311; cf. K. Kraft, "Das Silbermedallion Constantins des Grossen mit dem Christusmonogramm auf dem Helm," *Jahrbuch für Numismatik und Geldgeschichte*, 5/6 (1954/55), 151–178. Alföldi argues that "the presence of the 'immortale signum' on these public documents is decisive and could not have occured without the initiative or consent of the ruler." The validity of this interpretation has recently been questioned by P. Bruun in the selection printed in the present book and in his article "The Christian Signs on the Coins of Constantine," *Arctos*, n.s. 3 (1962), 5–35. On the pagan symbols and sentiments which continued to decorate Constantine's coinage long after 312, see Bruun, "The Disappearance of Sol from the Coins of Constantine," *Arctos*, n.s. 2 (1958), 15–37. Basing his argument on a collation of literary and numismatic evidence, Bruun has also challenged the traditional date of the battle at the Milvian Bridge. In his opinion, the battle was fought on October 28, 311, not 312 ("The Battle of the Milvian Bridge; The Date Reconsidered," *Hermes* 88 [1960], 361–370); for a critique of this hypothesis, see M. R. Alföldi and D. Kienast, "Zu P. Bruuns Datierung der Schlacht an der Milvischen Brücke," *Jahr-*

buch für Numismatik und Geldgeschichte, 11 (1961), 33–41.

Not infrequently objets d'art and monumental architecture, like the coinage, provide data not found in the literary texts. Three objects are especially important for the analysis of Constantine's religious thinking: the Arch of Constantine, the statue set up in the Roman Forum, and the labarum. The arch, which depicts among other things the battle of the Milvian Bridge, uniquely indicates Constantine's public attitude toward the events of 312 shortly after his victory (it was completed between 313 and 315). In an inscription on the base of the monument the victory is said—probably with Constantine's approval—to have been achieved instinctu divinitatis mentis magnitudine, "by the prompting of the divinity and the emperor's own greatness of mind." For the full text of the inscription, see the magnificent study of the arch by H. P. L'Orange and A. von Gerkan, Der Spätantike Bildsschmuck des Konstantinsbogen (Berlin, 1939); the historian will find less of interest in B. Berenson's morphological study, The Arch of Constantine (London, 1954). According to Eusebius, a statue of Constantine was erected in the Roman Forum by order of the Senate soon after the defeat of Maxentius; in his right hand Constantine held the "salutary symbol," which Eusebius and the author of the Life identify as a cross. H. Grégoire, however, argues that this was merely a cavalry vexillum, which had the shape of a cross ("La statue de Constantin et le signe de la Croix," L'Antiquité Classique, 1 [1932], 135–143). On the relationship of Eusebius' "salutary symbol" and the "signum dei" mentioned in the panegyric of 313, see J. Gagé, "La 'virtus' de Constantin a propos d'une inscription disçutée," Revue des Études Latines 12 (1934), 398–405; M. R. Alföldi, "Signum Deae. Die Kaiserzeitlichen Vorganger des Reichsapfels," Jahrbuch für Numismatik und Geldgeschichte, 11 (1961), 19–32; and C. Ligota, "Constantiniana," Journal of the Warburg and Courtauld Institutes, 26 (1963), 178–192. A good résumé of the controversy concerning the form and meaning of the labarum, the demonstrably Christian symbol described in the Life and perhaps in Lactantius' pamphlet, is pro-

vided by H. I. Marrou, "Autour du monogramme constantinien," Mélanges offerts à E. Gilson (Paris, 1959), pp. 403–414; cf. also R. Egger, "Das Labarum, die Kaiserstandarte der Spätantike, Sitzungsberichte der Akademie der Wissenschaften Wien 234 (1960), 1–26.

Such are the sources of information which the student of Constantine's religious behavior may exploit. How he employs this evidence will be determined by his general historical concepts, his skill in selecting, arranging, and assessing discrete data, and the range of his creative imagination. The cornerstone of the political interpretation, as we have seen, is an attack on the reliability of the Life of Constantine. Burckhardt and Grégoire argue that belief in the genuineness of Constantine's conversion to Christianity cannot be sustained once the testimony of the Life has been discredited. This critique was enough for Burckhardt, but Grégoire (in the selection printed above and in his later article "La vision de Constantin 'liquidée,'" Byzantion, 14 (1939), 341–351) expands the investigation through an analysis of the pagan vision reported by the panegyrist of 310. His thesis that the Christian vision was nothing more than a Christianized version of the pagan vision in Gaul, echoed by Hatt in the present volume, is essentially accepted by K. Hönn, Konstantin der Grosse (2d edition, Leipzig, 1945), who suggests that Constantine used the pagan-Christian visions, the Christogram on coinage, and the labarum as ideological weapons in his final war with Licinius.

An assessment of this pagan vision of 310 is also the basis of the syncretic interpretation. For W. Seston (p. 374 of his article "La Vision paienne de 310 et les origines du chrisme constantinien," Annuaire de l'Institut de Philologie et d'histoire Orientales et Slaves, 4 (1936), 373–395), Grégoire's analysis of the pagan vision supplied "a fresh approach to the religious history of Constantine's reign, for the vision of the Milvian Bridge, since it is no longer unique, has lost much of its miraculous quality." In Seston's view Constantine's efforts to establish a syncretic religion, in which traditional polytheism, philosophic monotheism, and Christianity could live in harmony, were misunderstood by later Christians, who created the "legend" of Constantine's conversion. See his article "L'Opinion paienne et la conversion de Constantin," *Revue d'histoire et de philosophie religieuses,* 16 (1936), 250–264; cf. also the slightly modified version of this hypothesis in A. Brasseur, "Les deux visions de Constantin," *Latomus,* 5 (1946), 35–40. The pagan vision is also the focus of an article by P. Orgels, "La première vision de Constantin (310) et la temple d'Apollon à Nîmes," *Bulletin de la Classe des lettres et des Sciences Morales et politiques,* Académie Royale de Belgique, 5th series 34 (1948), 176–208. Relying primarily on the testimony of the pagan panegyrists, Orgels concludes that Constantine consistently endeavored to establish a syncretic religion for the Roman state. On the Apollonian vision, also see E. Galletier, "La mort de Maximien d'après le panegyrique de 310 et la vision de Constantin au temple d'Apollon," *Revue des Études Anciennes,* 52 (1950), 288–299.

The majority of scholars today reject both the political and the syncretic interpretations and believe that Constantine sincerely adopted the Christian faith. Among the notable proponents of this view, in addition to the authors of the selections printed above, are J.-R. Palanque, *Constantin le Grand,* Collections Hommes d'État 1 (Paris, 1936), pp. 335–420; H. Doerries, *Konstantin der Grosse* (Stuttgart,

1959); and J. Vogt, *Constantin der Grosse und sein Jahrhundert* (2d edition, Munich, 1960). The possible influence of Bishop Ossius of Cordoba, who was a member of Constantine's entourage in 312, is discussed by V. C. de Clercq, *Ossius of Cordoba* (Catholic University of America, Studies in Christian Antiquity, 13, Washington, 1954). A "scientific" alternative to A. H. M. Jones' meteorological interpretation of Constantine's vision is advanced by F. Heiland in "Die Astronomische Deutung der Vision Konstantins," *Sondervertrag im Zeiss-Planetarium Jena* (October, 1948). According to Heiland, Constantine's vision was produced by the conjunction of the planets Saturn, Mars, and Jupiter within the zodiacal sign of Capricorn. These planets "inscribed" a cross in the heavens, which would have been visible in the Italian sky around October 28, 312. Heiland's calculations were checked by J. Gagé ("Le 'signum astrologique de Constantin et le millénarisme de 'Roma Aeterna,'" *Revue d'histoire et de philosophie religieuses,* 31 (1951), 181–223), who dates the "vision" to October 10–15, rather than October 28. Gagé's revision of Heiland's calculations is confirmed by B. Tuckerman, *Planetary, Lunar and Solar Positions A.D. 2 to A.D. 1649 at Five-Day and Ten-day Intervals,* in *Memoirs of the American Philosophical Society* 59 (1964), 174.